W9-CLQ-739

DIGNITY

DIGNITY

Its History and Meaning

MICHAEL ROSEN

HARVARD UNIVERSITY PRESS
Cambridge, Massachusetts, and London, England
2012

Library of Congress Cataloging-in-Publication Data

Rosen, Michael, 1952–
Dignity : its history and meaning / Michael Rosen.
p.   cm.
Includes bibliographical references (p.   ) and index.
ISBN 978-0-674-06443-0 (alk. paper)
1. Dignity.   2. Respect for persons.   I. Title.

BJ1533.R42R67   2012
179.7—dc23   2011032502

For Nancy Rosenblum
With affection, gratitude, and respect

CONTENTS

PREFACE

"So tell me," my friend Christopher McCrudden, the distinguished human rights lawyer, said one day over coffee, "what do philosophers have to say about 'dignity'?" I had read the novels of C. P. Snow and Michael Innes, and I always imagined that the air of Oxford Senior Common Rooms would be crackling with interdisciplinary exchanges. But, alas, if that kind of thing was going on, it had not been coming my way. So here was my chance! I must admit, though, that our conversation did not get off to the best start: "Er, not very much that I know about—Kant perhaps?" I replied.

Fortunately, Christopher proved a persistent (as well as tolerant) questioner, and the results of my further thinking (including many more conversations with him) are now in your hands. But before I thank those who helped to shape and correct my ideas, let me say something about the way that this book is presented.

It is often said that philosophy these days is not accessible to the general reader. This is obviously a matter for regret. If it is important that an educated person should have some understanding of the scientific knowledge on which our civilization relies (I have no doubt that it is), how much more so that she should have a conceptual framework within which to place that knowledge and some reflectively articulated principles by which to guide her action? In ethics and political life, issues of philosophical principle press on us whether we like it or not. When it is a question of deciding what action is right or whether to support a political proposal or arrangement, we must all decide for ourselves—even if, in the end, we decide to follow the direction of some authority (the case for doing which, by the way, is much less straightforward than for following the experts in a technical matter). So there is certainly a good reason for philosophy to try to reach an audience beyond its professional boundaries.

But that does not mean that it is possible. Perhaps the gap between philosophy and the general reader is inevitable. We don't imagine that someone could understand genetics or astrophysics without specialist training—why should philosophy be different? It may be that this gap is the price we have to pay for progress.

Writing philosophy accessibly is certainly not easy. It is not that philosophy is intrinsically more difficult than other academic disciplines (they are all quite difficult enough, thank you!) but that philosophy is peculiarly resistant to one kind of popularization. As the many brilliant writers on science now active show, it is possible to present the results of scientific research (and even mathematics) in ways that don't require the reader to be able to follow the technical details that underlie them or to check for herself how those results were achieved. But to describe philosophy's most advanced positions (even assuming that we agree what they are) in this way without also giving an account of the reasons for adopting them would be a complete waste of time. Philosophical arguments (good ones, at any rate!) make it possible for us to support rationally convictions that we have formed outside of philosophy or to challenge our complacency about things that we otherwise take for granted. They are the essential part of the subject—philosophy without its arguments is like football without a ball.

We cannot usefully present philosophy without actually doing it, then—and yet to do philosophy presupposes a great deal. Philosophy is a holistic discipline. All of its theories and problems relate, in the end, to all the rest. So to address one problem we must have—if not *resolved* all of the others, at least be prepared to "put them on hold" for the time being. Not least, we (that is, author and reader) must have some shared understanding of what constitutes a good philosophical argument, and this (as philosophers know well, although non-philosophers are often surprised, and sometimes even outraged, to learn) is itself a matter of acute controversy. For a rough analogy, compare the philosopher with a chess player. If her argument were to be conclusive, the philosopher would have to be able, when she "makes a move" (that is, puts forward an argument or advocates a position), to meet all the counter-moves that might be made, and all the counter-moves to her own counter-moves—in fact, to address the whole exponentially expanding tree-structure of possibilities that lies beneath that single move. But not just that—here is where chess and philosophy differ—she must be prepared to justify why the game should be played according to just these rules and not other ones. So the ideal of completeness in philosophical argument is, in practice, wholly chimerical and the philosopher faces a repeated series of uncomfortable choices about what to take for granted and what to put on the table for debate at any stage. On the one hand, there must be shared assumptions between an author and her readers for argument to get going at all; on the other, challenging assumptions is precisely what philosophy (at least, philosophy at its best) is all about.

In consequence, the idea of "proof" in the strict sense has very little place in philosophy. Philosophical positions can rarely be demonstrated, because the alternatives to them are rarely wholly refuted—gaps can almost always be plugged, even if the intellectual price of doing so may seem to reasonably open-minded people absurdly high. But this does not mean that philosophy is not a matter of rational argument. John Stuart Mill makes exactly this point in *Utilitarianism*. Although, he admits, questions of ultimate ends (and, hence, the justification of utilitarianism) are not amenable to proof, "There is a larger meaning of the word proof, in which this question is as amenable to it as any other of the disputed questions of philosophy. The subject is within the cognisance of the rational faculty; and neither does that faculty deal with it solely in the way of intuition. Considerations may be presented capable of determining the intellect either to give or withhold its assent to the doctrine; and this is equivalent to proof." To put it more bluntly, just because we can't reach a mathematical ideal of proof, we shouldn't throw up our hands and conclude that philosophy is no more than personal preference. We can give reasons for and against positions, reasons that carry weight even if they're not conclusive.

These, then, are some reasons of principle why philosophy is so hard to practice in an accessible way. They also, incidentally, help to explain its tendency to fracture into "schools" and "traditions" that talk past one another. The different traditions disagree not just about foreground substance, but also (what is more difficult to deal with) about the background assumptions that must be presupposed to get philosophical discourse going.

Yet there are also some bad reasons why philosophy today is inaccessible, most of them to do with over-professionalization (I am thinking here of the English-speaking world). My guess is that the dominance of the sciences in the academy, with their emphasis on peer review, has a good deal to do with it. Of course, there is a strong justification for papers in scientific journals being impersonally written and subjected to the disciplines of critical peer review—nothing is more important in experimental science than establishing solid, repeatable results—but the idea of extending this to philosophy is questionable. Admittedly, accountability brings benefits in philosophy as well. (I wonder how far the pretentious, uncritical style of much contemporary "Continental"

philosophy is a result of the lack of such discipline.) But
something is lost too. If, for the reasons outlined above,
the idea of completeness in philosophical arguments is
unattainable, the attempt to be "rigorous" can lead to a
defensive tendency to reduce ambitions and to protect
some tiny piece of ground against the possible objections
of those closest to oneself in background and outlook
(one's natural peer reviewers). What is lost is not just ac-
cessibility but also the willingness to call into question
basic assumptions (one's own and others'), which is
precisely what, for many of us, the point of doing philosophy was in the first place. Much contemporary philosophy takes place in an atmosphere of what can only
be called (however historically unfair that label might
be) scholasticism.

There are several reasons why it seemed to me that a
more informal approach was in place for this book. One
obvious one is that, as my conversation with McCrudden
makes clear, it is not just philosophers who are interested
in dignity. If the price of making what I have to say more
approachable for such readers is to cut short some more
inward-looking discussions, it seems to me that the trade-
off is worth making. Moreover—my initial response was
not wholly mistaken—there does not exist a large, systematic body of contemporary philosophical literature
on dignity whose arguments require a response.

However, not every topic I shall deal with has been so
neglected. I shall enter two (connected) areas of discussion—
the interpretation of Kant's moral philosophy, and the
character of moral duty—that are as densely populated

as any region of philosophy. What I have to say about Kant and the idea of duty disagrees with a great deal of what has been written on the subject. In this case my reason for taking a less comprehensive approach is just the opposite. To revert to my chess analogy, I am in the situation of someone who wants to propose making a radically unorthodox move at a frequently reached point in the game. Of course, I think that there are good reasons for the move I want to make, and I shall try to give them. But I shall do so in a frankly exploratory spirit and confine myself to those reasons that seem to me most compelling without trying to demonstrate comprehensively that more conventional alternatives are misguided. If you see things differently and I fail to convince you, so be it—but I hope, at least, you will appreciate the reasons I take the view that I do.

I have referred to this book as a work of philosophy—and rightly so, for the topics I have just mentioned are as central to philosophy as any that one could think of. But, in fact, I prefer the label "political theory." This is not because I think that political philosophy and political theory are wholly different subjects. On the contrary, in my view everything that is called "political philosophy" is to be found in political theory and, so far as they overlap, there is no important difference between the two. But there are those who think that the term "philosophy" should be reserved for theorizing that is purely "analytical" or "conceptual" or "a priori," and this book contains material that (on any understanding of those terms) is not that. My own view of philosophy is actually much broader.

In my opinion, our best way of proceeding (in political philosophy, at least) is to be prepared to allow facts into our normative reflection and use history as part of our conceptual analysis. But this is something that I assume here rather than argue for. Political theory, at any rate, suffers from no such closed-borders policy—it is the oasis where the caravans meet—so "political theory" it is, please.

I was fortunate to be invited to present my ideas about dignity as the Benedict Lectures at Boston University in 2007. The present text is a revised and expanded version of those lectures. I am extremely grateful to my hosts, Aaron Garrett and James Schmidt. I have tried to keep the informality and personal tone of the lecture format in the hope that it will make what I have to say more accessible (and, perhaps, more entertaining).

In doing so, one decision to be made was what to do about footnotes. Now there is a lot to be said for footnotes (Anthony Grafton in his wonderful book on the subject has said almost all of it), but one cannot pretend that they make a piece of writing easier for the reader to follow. Their employment in philosophy to add in second thoughts and counter objections is not new (Kant did so pretty much compulsively), but I think that—perhaps as a product of that defensive impulse to try to block every alternative avenue I mentioned above or simply because word processors have made them so easy to create—they are greatly over-used nowadays. Nevertheless, of course, claims should be capable of being backed up, and readers have every right to check things for themselves. In the end, I have restricted myself to a small number of endnotes (identified by page numbers and a few key words), which can, I hope, be ignored without substantive loss.

Other audiences who responded to this material were at: the Murphy Center, Tulane University; the Humboldt University, Berlin; the University of California at Berkeley (where I used some of the ideas to be found here in replying to Jeremy Waldron's splendid Tanner Lectures); and the Safra Center for Ethics, Harvard University. Johann Frick was an invaluable research assistant who, as well as helping me identify relevant material, gave me the benefit of his own superb critical responses (not all of which, I fear, I have met). For individual comments and suggestions I am especially grateful to: Ewa Atanassow, Eric Beerbohm, Josh Cherniss, G. A. Cohen, Maximilian de Gaynesford, Alison Denham, Wai Chee Dymock, Dina Emundts, Hannah Ginsborg, Anand Giridharadas, Sam Goldman, James Griffin, Dieter Grimm, Rolf Horstmann, Nahomi Ichino, Martin Jay, Alexander Key, Tarunabh Khaitan, Manfred Kuehn, Rae Langton, Harvey Mansfield, Christopher McCrudden, Frank Michelman, Sophia Moreau, Eric Nelson, Brian O'Connor, Lena Rohrbach, Nancy Rosenblum, Michael Sandel, Eric Southworth, Lucas Stanczyk, John Tasioulas, Richard Tuck, Jeremy Waldron, and three acute, but anonymous, readers for Harvard University Press. I cannot close without thanking my editor, Mike Aronson. His patience and good humor have been everything that an author could wish for—I only hope that he feels that the result bears out his enthusiasm.

REFERENCES AND ABBREVIATIONS

In-text references to Kant are made to the standard German edition in the following way. The abbreviation *"Ak."* (standing for *Akademie Edition*) is followed by two numbers separated by a colon, the first of which stands for the volume number, the second the page. Thus *"Ak.* 4:436" refers to *Akademie,* volume 4, page 436 (in fact, a page of the *Groundwork to the Metaphysics of Morals*). I will generally mention the English name of the work in question in the text. This system should work for readers with no access to the German, since most English translations (including the now-standard Cambridge Edition of the Works of Immanuel Kant in Translation) reprint the *Akademie* page numbers in their margins.

Papal documents have been retrieved in their official English versions from the Vatican website. The numbers given in brackets in the text are paragraph numbers in the original. Extracts from decisions of the German Constitutional Court (Bundesverfassungsgericht) are referenced as BVerfGE followed by the file reference.

DIGNITY

I

"THE SHIBBOLETH OF ALL EMPTY-HEADED MORALISTS"

I. Humbug?

Schopenhauer, the Ebenezer Scrooge of nineteenth-century philosophy, took a characteristically jaundiced view of talk of human dignity: "That expression, *dignity of man,* once uttered by Kant, afterward became the shibboleth of all the perplexed and empty-headed moralists who concealed behind that imposing expression their lack of any real basis of morals, or, at any rate, of one that had any meaning. They cunningly counted on the fact that their readers would be glad to see themselves invested with such a *dignity* and would accordingly be quite satisfied with it." Is Schopenhauer right? Is the talk of "dignity" mere humbug—a pompous facade, flattering to our self-esteem but without any genuine substance behind it?

Schopenhauer's criticism is troubling when we think how important the word "dignity" has become in contemporary political and ethical discussion. Dignity is central to modern human rights discourse, the closest that we have to an internationally accepted framework for the normative regulation of political life, and it is embedded in numerous constitutions, international conventions, and declarations. It plays a vital role, for example, in two fundamental documents from the late 1940s, the United Nations' Universal Declaration of Human Rights (1948) and the Grundgesetz (Basic Law) of the Federal Republic of Germany (1949). This is apparent from its prominent position in each text. The very first sentence of Article 1 of the Universal Declaration reads: "All human beings are born free and equal in dignity and rights"; while Article 1 of the Grundgesetz states: "Human dignity is inviolable. To respect it and protect it is the duty of all state power. The German people therefore acknowledge inviolable and inalienable human rights as the basis of every community, of peace and of justice in the world."

We should not infer from the close connection between "dignity" and human rights in such texts that talk about dignity is simply a piece of liberal piety, however. In August 2006, President Ahmadinejad of Iran (whose piety, I think it is fair to say, is more apparent than his liberalism) sent a strange letter to the German chancellor, Angela Merkel. It was written, to quote Ahmadinejad's own words, from the conviction that it is "the common responsibility of all people with faith in God to defend *human dignity* and worth and to prevent violation of their rights and their humiliation, proceeding from the conviction that we are all created by the Almighty and that he has bestowed *dignity* upon us all and that no one has any special privileges over the other." Ahmadinejad is very fond of the discourse of dignity. Shortly after his letter to Merkel, he rejected calls for Iran to subject its nuclear program to international control. Iran would not be intimidated by the West, he asserted, but would continue on its "path of dignity."

"Dignity" appears frequently in faith-based ethical discourse. Although not the rhetorical property of any single religion, it is most prominent in Catholic thought. In *Evangelium Vitae,* the encyclical issued in March 1995 by Pope John Paul II to address questions of contraception, abortion, and the use of modern reproductive technologies (25.iii. 1995), the word is used no fewer than fifty-six times. Although there is no single authoritative source for Protestant doctrine, dignity is also a common theme in contemporary Protestant writing. Reinhold Niebuhr, for example, tells us that the dignity of man "consists of a unique freedom which is able not only to transcend the 'laws' of nature or of reason to which classical and modern culture would bind it, but also to defy and outrage the very structure of man's existence"; while the celebrated German theologian Jürgen Moltmann, author of *On Human Dignity,* writes: "The dignity of each and every human being is grounded in [its] objective likeness of God" (a sentence that could just as easily have come from the pen of John Paul II or Benedict XVI).

It is striking in how many contexts one encounters the word—here are a few personal examples. As I write, I have in front of me a piece by the *New York Times* columnist David Brooks called "In Search of Dignity," in which he regrets the passing of what he calls "the dignity code" of reticence and self-restraint from American public life (he points to the dignified figure of President Obama as a hopeful counter to the trend). In 2008 the Ig Nobel Prize for Peace was awarded to "The Swiss Federal Ethics Committee on Non-Human Biotechnology (ECNH) and the citizens of Switzerland for adopting the legal principle that plants have dignity" (more on this below). A recently deceased former England football manager who had presided (as England managers do) over a heartbreaking defeat was described in his obituary in *The Times* as behaving with "stoicism and dignity" when (as is equally predictable) he was reviled and insulted in the popular press. More disturbingly, during the Pinochet years in Chile, a fundamentalist religious colony of German expatriates, run by a former Evangelical preacher (and pedophile), was used by the secret police for the torture and murder of opponents of the regime. The community's name was Colonia Dignidad. (I did not open the spam e-mail I received recently whose subject header invited me to "Become the man of huge dignity," but I think that I can make a good guess at its content.)

And yet, when we look at the concept of dignity from the viewpoint of philosophy, the situation is quite different. Although, apparently, no significant area of human life—from sport to architecture, from war to sexuality—is without its attendant philosophical specialists, conferences, and journals these days, the lack of philosophical interest in the concept of dignity is striking. That superbly comprehensive reference work, the *Routledge Encyclopedia of Philosophy,* for example, contains no entry under "dignity." Where they notice the concept of dignity at all, the attitude of philosophers is frequently dismissive or hostile. In 2002 the philosopher Ruth Macklin published an editorial in the *British Medical Journal* whose headline pretty much sums up its content: "Dignity is a useless concept. It means no more than respect for persons or their autonomy." According to Macklin, "appeals to dignity are either vague restatements of other, more precise notions or mere slogans that add nothing to the understanding of the topic."

For Macklin (like Schopenhauer) the concept of dignity is redundant at best—any content it has comes from another value, autonomy. Such a view of dignity is common among the relatively few contemporary philosophers writing in English who make mention of dignity. I take it that it is James Griffin's view when he writes that "autonomy is a major part of rational agency, and rational agency constitutes what philosophers have often called, with unnecessary obscurity, the 'dignity' of the person." And it was, it seems clear, also the view of the late Joel Feinberg: "Respect for persons may simply be respect for their rights, so that there cannot be one without the other; and what is called 'human dignity' may simply be the recognizable capacity to assert claims. To respect a person, then, or to think of him as possessed of human dignity simply is to think of him as a potential maker of claims." For Feinberg, to respect the dignity of persons means just to respect persons, and we respect persons in exactly the same way as we respect the law. Just as we respect the speed limit by driving below 50 kph, so we respect persons by respecting their rights—not subjecting them to torture, arbitrary arrest, and so on and so forth.

The idea that dignity is redundant and could be replaced by another, more fundamental value may not be the only reason to be skeptical about its use in contemporary moral discourse, however. Another possibility is that, although there is a distinct value of dignity, it is not a universal moral value, as the Universal Declaration and the Grundgesetz would have it. Instead of dignity being a characteristic that all human beings have simply in virtue of being human, dignity is something more modest and restricted: an aesthetic quality that manifests itself in human behavior or (if that is something different) a virtue. On this view, some people (at least) are dignified (at least some of the time) but dignity is not a universal and inalienable property of human beings, something that gives a foundational reason for their having equal basic entitlements in relation to the actions of the state and fellow members of the human race (or, to put that mouthful in more simple terms: *human rights*).

Finally, skepticism about dignity can take a third form—the idea that dignity has no coherent meaning of its own but is given content by a range of extraneous political, social, and religious convictions for which the word itself functions as a mere receptacle. The variations in the use of the term "dignity" are undeniable. We can find dignity being invoked by advocates of flatly opposed moral positions. Where John Paul II, for example, believed that dignity requires the inviolability of all human life from the moment of conception to the expiration of all vital functions, the well-known Swiss organization Dignitas is famous for assisting those who wish to "die with dignity" to end their own lives. The Catholic Church claims that its affirmation of the dignity of every human being is compatible with its teaching that "homosexual acts are intrinsically disordered." Dignity USA, on the other hand, is an organization that, in its own words, "envisions and works for a time when Gay, Lesbian, Bisexual and Transgender Catholics are affirmed and experience dignity through the integration of their spirituality with their sexuality, and as beloved persons of God participate fully in all aspects of life within the Church and Society."

Or consider the case of Ms. Geisy Arruda. As reported by the BBC, Ms. Arruda, a student at Bandeirante University in Sao Paolo, "provoked jeers and insults" from her fellow students when she attended class in a very short red dress. She was expelled from the university for showing "a flagrant lack of respect for ethical principles, academic dignity and morality." The university reversed its decision, however, after much media publicity, and Ms. Arruda's lawyers brought a case for damages to compensate for her, as they put it, "trampled dignity."

The interesting question, then, is not: are the uses of "dignity" variable?—who could deny it?—but why is this so? If the meaning of a term is confusing simply because the ideas motivating it are complex, that should not deter philosophers, should it? Isn't the clarification of confusion (at least an important part of) our proper business? I am going to show that there are indeed systematic reasons behind the different (and often opposed) uses of the term. To untangle the idea of dignity, the best way,

I think, is to reach back to its roots, and these—like all concepts of significant interest in political life—are historical. But before I do that, let me say a little more about my project in this book.

In the rest of this chapter, I shall trace some of the different senses in which the term has been used. One very common way in which writers present the history of dignity is as part of what I call an "expanding circle" narrative. From this perspective, the quality of dignity, once the property of a social elite, has, like the idea of rights, been extended outward and downward until it has come to apply to all human beings. This is all part of that great, long process by which the fundamental equality of human beings has come to be generally accepted. There is something right (and appealing) about this picture, yet what it leaves out is also important if we want to understand how the word "dignity" is used nowadays—and why it is the source of so much disagreement. History shows the existence of significant distinct strands in the meaning of dignity, strands that come together and move apart at different times. An important feature of this history, but one that is hard to square with the expanding-circle narrative, is that dignity has not always been seen as something that is restricted to human beings alone—whether to human beings as such or some special, elite group of them. Another is that in the nineteenth century the Catholic Church used the term "dignity" as part of a fiercely anti-egalitarian discourse. The fact that the idea of human dignity should later have come to be associated in Catholic thinking, as elsewhere, with equality and human rights represents a sharp, important (and, to my mind, very welcome) intellectual change, not just a further step along a long, straight road to democracy.

The second chapter looks at some ways in which "dignity" has been used in recent legal discourse. Encouraged by the kind of statements that figure so prominently in the Universal Declaration and the Grundgesetz, there is a natural tendency to imagine dignity as an "inner, transcendental kernel"—something intangible that all human beings carry inalienably inside them that underlies the moral claims that they have just by being human (and that states have the duty to uphold). If this is what dignity is supposed to be, it isn't surprising that so many philosophers are so tetchy about it. Of course, Kantians and Catholics *do* have accounts of what this inner, transcendental kernel amounts to—but they involve wider, metaphysical commitments that (to put it mildly) not everyone will accept. Moreover, attempts to apply this foundational conception of dignity in practice (in Germany, for example) fall short, so far as I can see, of showing the kind of cogent route from principle to application that we would hope for. In fact, I shall give reasons to think that legal decisions allegedly based on this inner transcendental kernel are given substance by the importation of one or more of the other senses of "dignity" (for example, that of behaving in a dignified way or being treated in a way that expresses respect for one's humanity) that I will distinguish in this first chapter.

Finally, the idea that dignity involves the expression of respect for the value of humanity raises a philosophical puzzle that is (or so I believe) of great interest, depth, and importance. Why should we have a duty to express respect for humanity when no one is benefited by our fulfillment of that duty—something that at least seems to be the case when we treat the dead "with dignity"? In Chapter 3, I shall propose a very radical solution to that puzzle, one that advocates an approach to ethics that is quite different from those that dominate current thinking on the subject.

A theme that runs through all three chapters is how best to understand Kant's view of dignity (and with good reason—my initial response to McCrudden wasn't wholly wrong, I think). Kant played an important role historically in connecting dignity with the idea of all human beings having unconditional, intrinsic value, and it is by reference to Kant (particularly his famous statement that human beings should always be treated as ends and never as means only) that attempts have been made to turn the principle of respect for dignity into practical moral and legal decisions, so there is no way round him if we want to understand the history of the term, its conceptual structure, and its application. What is more, I shall argue that Kant's moral philosophy, when properly understood, actually represents a challenge to a currently ruling orthodoxy about the nature of morality that makes the puzzle of Chapter 3 so difficult to resolve. I don't myself think that that means that we should accept Kant's "Platonism" (as I shall call it) about morality, but the independent place it gives to the idea of moral duty seems very persuasive to me (and, if all goes well, when I have finished, I hope, to you too).

II. Cicero and After

Historical phenomena rarely derive from a single source, bubbling up out of the ground like the spring at the start of a river, and so it is with "dignity." "Dignity" originated as a concept that denoted high social status and the honors and respectful treatment that are due to someone who occupied that position. Terms to express similar conceptions exist in most languages, including ancient ones. Kind informants have told me that such terms exist in Chinese, Japanese, Korean, Arabic, and Persian, for example. There are four uses of "dignity" in the King James translation of the Hebrew Bible, although they render three different Hebrew words. All three apparently also contain the sense of "elevation" or "majesty." Interestingly, however, in modern Ivrit, I am told, the preferred term for dignity is not one of these status-related words but "B'Tselem," which comes from Genesis 1:27 ("So God created man in his own image, in the image of God created he him," in the King James translation). B'Tselem is also the name of an admirable human rights organization: the Israeli Information Center for Human Rights in the Occupied Territories.

Yet even in its very early stages, the idea of dignity in the Western tradition went beyond merely ascribing to individuals an elevated status in a particular social order. This is apparent in that immensely influential ancient text, Cicero's *De Officiis* (On Duties). Elsewhere in his works, Cicero uses *dignitas* as a conventional status term. For example, he uses the phrase *cum dignitate otium* (leisure with dignity) to characterize how the *optimi* (the best men) in a well-ordered republic should aim to live. *Dignitas* here evidently just means something like "honor" or an "honored place." In *De Officiis*, however, Cicero considers the dignity that human beings have solely because they are human, not animals. He writes: "in every investigation into the nature of duty, it is vitally necessary for us to remember always how vastly superior is man's nature to that of cattle and other animals: their only thought is for bodily satisfactions. . . . Man's mind, on the contrary, is developed by study and reflection. . . . From this we may learn that sensual pleasure is wholly unworthy of the dignity of the human race." The Stoics taught that human beings should see themselves as "citizens of the world," and Cicero's use of "dignity" in this passage is surely a continuation of this thought. What is at issue is not just what position some individual or group occupies in relation to other human beings in a particular society, but what position human beings as a whole occupy in the order of the universe. So, right from the outset, dignity has been transposed and extended into a way of saying something about human beings as such.

The status aspect of dignity is one fundamental thread running through the history of the term, but another aspect of its meaning that goes back to the Roman world should also be introduced now, although it will become of political significance only much later. The term *dignitas* functioned in Latin as part of a critical vocabulary in relation to art and, particularly, rhetoric. *Dignitas* and its relative, *gravitas,* were used (notably, by Cicero himself in his *De Oratore*) to characterize speech that was weighty and majestic, in contrast to discourse that was light and charming (which was referred to by the words *gratias* and *venustus*). And (as in our own modern usage) the term was applied not just to the manner of a speech but to the speaker him—it always was "him"—self. We have here the roots of the association of the idea of dignity with what is "dignified" in manner.

The use of "dignity" as a status term continues into the Christian era. Here it is, for example, in a very famous letter written by Pope Gelasius I to Emperor Anastasius in 494 that discusses the relationship between Church and State:

> There are two powers by which the world is chiefly governed, the sacred authority of the priesthood and the royal power. Of these the responsibility of the priests is more weighty in so far as they will answer for the kings of men themselves at the divine judgement. You know, most clement son, that, although you take precedence over all mankind in dignity, never-theless you piously bow the neck to those who have charge of divine affairs and seek from them the means of your salvation.

Clearly, what Gelasius means by "dignity" is the em-peror's worldly status *(potestas),* which he contrasts with the (ultimately more important) divine *auctoritas* of the Church and the emperor's standing before God. There is a permanent tension in the Christian attitude toward this status conception of "dignity," however. The idea of a reversal of status—"the last shall be first"—is a fundamental trope (actually, I would say, *the* fundamental trope) in Christian social thought, and it can point in two directions. Sometimes, as in Gelasius's letter, it leads to the rejection of the value of dignity (understood as worldly status) in the name of other, spiritual values. Yet at other times religious humility itself is identified as the true dignity. Ruskin expresses this basic thought beautifully in his essay "The Nature of Gothic." Christianity, he writes, "[recognizes] in small things as well as great, the individual value of every soul. But it not only recognizes its value; it confesses its imperfection, in only bestowing dignity upon the acknowledgment of unworthiness." (The words of the centurion when Jesus offered to go to his house to cure his daughter—*"Domine, non sum dignus"* (Lord, I am not worthy)—are repeated by the priest as part of the Catholic mass.)

Cicero's extension of dignity from a matter of the position of individuals in particular societies to the place occupied by human beings within the wider order of reality is taken up again in the Renaissance, most famously in Pico della Mirandola's oration known as *De Dignitate Hominis*. (I say "known as" because the title, it has now been established, was given to the work only after Pico's death.) In his oration Pico gives an account of human nature that was to be in many ways seminal for the self-understanding of human beings in the modern world. The distinctiveness of man, he claims, lies precisely in the way that human beings do not simply fulfill a pre-ordained role. On the contrary, man *chooses* his own destiny, for God has given him the capacity to shape himself according to a range of possibilities not available to other creatures. Pico's oration might seem to open a relatively clear path toward the use of dignity we find in modern human rights documents. "Dignity" goes from being a matter of the elevated status of a few persons in a particular society to being a feature of human beings in general, closely connected with their capacity for self-determination. But, in fact, this is only one strand in the development of the idea of dignity. If we are to understand the use of the term today (and the sources of its underlying conflicts), we need a more complex story.

In 1623 Francis Bacon published an expanded translation into Latin of his own book, the *Advancement of Learning,* under the title *De Dignitate et Augmentis Scientiarum.* One thing that is very striking is that the term *dignitas* is being applied here to an abstract entity—learning. Clearly, dignity cannot be a matter of social status, even in the extended sense in which human beings are members of the wider society of God's creation. In fact, the most immediately natural translation for *dignitate* in Bacon's title would be "worth" or "value." This is not the only sense in which Bacon uses "dignity." He writes, for example (at the beginning of his essay "Of Great Place"): "The rising into place is laborious, and by pains men come to greater pains; and it is sometimes base, and by indignities men come to dignities." As in Gelasius's letter to the emperor, "dignities" in this case are evidently a matter of high social status (a synonym for "place"), and the ironic point that he is making is that the behavior associated with arriving there is not itself "dignified." We can see here three quite different meanings—dignity as a valuable characteristic not restricted to human beings, dignity as high social status, and dignity as behavior with a certain respect-worthy character (or indignity as behavior lacking it)—co-existing in a single author in the early modern period, just as they seem to do today.

The use of "dignity" as an evaluative term of wider application is found in English as well as Latin in the seventeenth century. Milton in the preface to his 1644 essay "Of the Doctrine and Discipline of Divorce" asserts that the value of marriage lies in the character of the social relationship between men and women. He writes "God in the first ordaining of marriage, taught us to what end he did it, in words expressly implying the apt and cheerful conversation of man with woman, to comfort and refresh him against the evil of solitary life, not mentioning the purpose of generation till afterwards, as being but *a secondary end in dignity, though not in necessity*" (my emphasis). Milton is ascribing dignity not to human beings, or even to marriage as such, but to the purposes that marriage serves.

Such uses of "dignity" to ascribe a kind of value to something—possibly something quite abstract—are, in fact, deeply rooted. That most seminal of Catholic thinkers, St. Thomas Aquinas, gives us an explicit definition of dignity in his *Commentary on the Sentences* that says just that: "Dignity signifies something's goodness on account of itself." In other words, for Aquinas, "dignity" is a term for, as we would now put it, something's intrinsic value—the value that it has by occupying its appropriate place within God's creation, as revealed by Scripture and by natural law. (The fact that something is created by, and hence is dependent on, God, doesn't mean that it cannot have goodness "on account of itself," by the way; its goodness may still be intrinsic to it as the particular thing that it is, even though it is God who has made it to be that thing.) This sense of dignity as the intrinsic value of something that occupies its proper place is an important strand running through dignity discourse, particularly Catholic, and, in its light, matters look somewhat different than if we think of dignity as essentially a matter of social status. From this point of view, human beings do indeed have dignity, but dignity is not essentially restricted to human beings. The world is composed of many things, all of them ultimately created by God and thus having their own dignity. The important question becomes: What *kind* of dignity does any particular thing that has dignity have and in virtue of what does it have it?

So, if we return to Pico della Mirandola's oration, we can see it as giving an answer to the question *what kind* of dignity human beings have. *De Dignitate et Augmentis Scientarum* asks about the place and value of learning, and so on. Different things that have dignity have it in different ways, and they may have it for different reasons. Thus Pascal, in one of the most famous of his *Pensées,* agrees with Pico in seeing man as having a dignity elevated above the rest of nature, but his account of what it consists in is different:

> Man is only a reed, the weakest in nature, but he is a thinking reed. There is no need for the universe to take up arms to crush him: a vapour, a drop of water is enough to kill him. But even if the universe were to crush him, man would still be nobler than his slayer, because he knows that he is dying and the advantage the universe has over him. The universe knows none of this. Thus *all our dignity consists in thought.* (my emphasis)

In 1659 Bishop Bossuet preached a sermon, "Sur l'éminente dignité des pauvres dans l'Église" (On the eminent dignity of the poor in the Church). Bossuet was court preacher at the court of Louis Quatorze and, not surprisingly, no advocate of social equality. His attribution of "eminent dignity" to the poor is meant, not to attribute to them a status equal with (or even higher than) the nobility, but to assert their own distinctive value within a properly ordered hierarchy. Each alike has dignity, but what that dignity consists in is different for each. At this point let me put in a word or two in defense of the Swiss Federal Ethics Committee on Non-Human Biotechnology. The Ig Nobel prizes are awarded (by the journal *Annals of Improbable Research*) for achievements that "first make people laugh and then make them think," and it seems to me that attributing dignity to plants does just that. If the Federal Ethics Committee were asserting that plants have the same kind of dignity that humans do, then it would indeed be claiming something laughable. But if we take this Catholic tradition seriously, not all dignity is *human* dignity. Human dignity is only one (if extremely important) form of dignity. Perhaps plants have an intrinsic value to be defended too. At least (as the Ig Nobel Committee would wish) it is a point to think about.

III. Kant

Although the use of dignity in all three of the strands of meaning that I have distinguished so far was widespread through the seventeenth and eighteenth centuries, the concept played only a small role in political theory until the time of that thinker on whose giant shoulders the modern theory of human rights largely rests, Immanuel Kant. It is appropriate that Kant's thought about dignity should stand at the center of any historical account of dignity, for it has been the inspiration—rightly or wrongly—of very much of what has come later. Nevertheless, the role that dignity plays in Kant's ethical thinking is not straightforward (or, unfortunately, easy to explain).

The German word for dignity is *Würde,* a word that is closely related etymologically to *Wert,* the term for "worth" or "value." The adjectival form, *würdig,* means both "valuable" or "deserving"—as in "deserving of reward"—and "dignified." (There is a parallel here with Latin—*Domine, non sum dignus*—and English. "Worthy," which has, of course, the same root as *Würde,* has something of the same duality. We talk, for example, about "local worthies" or "dignitaries" as well as of "worthy winners.") The

German use of the word *Würde* in something like the same (somewhat ambiguous) way as it was used in English and Latin can be documented in that supremely influential source of modern German prose, Martin Luther. In his *On Christian Liberty*, Luther uses the word to characterize the spiritual condition of the true Christian:

> I can turn all things to the profit of my salvation; so that even the cross and death are compelled to serve me and to work together for my salvation. This is a lofty and eminent dignity [*eine hohe, ehrliche Würdigkeit*], a true and almighty dominion, a spiritual empire, in which there is nothing so good, nothing so bad, as not to work together for my good, if only I believe.

Now Kant himself actually uses the term *Würde* relatively infrequently, with the exception of a single work. But since that work is the *Groundwork to the Metaphysics of Morals* (1785)—by far the most widely known and studied of Kant's ethical writings—it is not surprising that the concept has come to be seen as having a central place in his thought.

Kant uses the word *Würde* sixteen times in the *Groundwork*. Most significantly, it is used four times (numbers 5–8) and explained in the following passage:

> In the kingdom of ends everything has either a *price* or a *dignity*. What has a price can be replaced by something else as its *equivalent;* what

on the other hand is raised above all price and
therefore admits of no equivalent has a dignity.

What is related to general human inclinations and needs has a *market price;* that which,
even without presupposing a need, conforms
with a certain taste, that is, with a delight in
the mere purposeless play of our mental powers
has a *fancy price;* but that which constitutes the
condition under which something can be an
end in itself has not merely a relative value, that
is, a price, but an inner value, that is *dignity.*

Now, morality is the condition under which
alone a rational being can be an end in itself,
since only through this is it possible to be a lawgiving member in the kingdom of ends. Hence
morality, and humanity insofar as it is capable
of morality, is that which alone has dignity.
(*Ak.* 4:434–435)

This dense and complex passage goes right to the heart
of Kant's view of morality. Clearly, he is distinguishing
between two kinds of value: those that are fungible (can
be substituted for) and those that have an "inner value"
and are "raised above all price," or that have, as he puts it
on the following page, "an unconditional, incomparable
value" (*Ak.* 4:436). Indeed, we could simply use that latter
phrase to replace most of Kant's uses of the term "dignity." So when Kant goes on to write that "*Autonomy* is
therefore the ground of the dignity of human nature"
(*Ak.* 4:436), we could just as easily read him as saying that

autonomy is the ground of human nature's unconditional, incomparable value.

Kant's core concept of dignity in the *Groundwork* as a
value that is "inner" and "unconditional" turns out to be
surprisingly similar to Aquinas's definition of dignity as
the goodness that something has "on account of itself."
Their views about what things the term applies to could
hardly be further apart, however. For Aquinas, many
things are good on account of themselves (indeed, arguably everything that has been created by God is good,
provided that it occupies its proper position in the order
of creation). "Dignity," for Kant, on the other hand, is a
quality of a class of valuable things that, as it turns out,
only has a single member: "morality, and humanity itself
insofar as it is capable of morality."

This may seem to be a somewhat complex and obscure
idea, but it is, in fact, important (and, to my knowledge,
not something that has been widely noticed), so here is a
comparison that may make it clearer. Imagine a professor declares that a piece of work by one of her students
is "prize-worthy." To say that the work is prize-worthy
is clearly to say that it is good, but it does not say what is
good about it. We know what it is for work to have substantive values—what it is for it to be well expressed, original, detailed, insightful, and so on. These are characteristics for which we have criteria. But we don't have
independent criteria for "prize-worthiness." On the contrary, the professor judges that the work is prize-worthy
because it has (some combination of) those more specific, valuable characteristics. So prize-worthiness is not

a substantive value but something that it derives from having those other qualities. Those qualities make prize-worthy work good in a different way from work that is (say) merely praiseworthy. Something like that is what I mean by saying that dignity, for Kant, is a *kind of* value rather than being a value itself.

Kant's discussion of dignity in the *Groundwork* leaves some difficult but philosophically important issues unaddressed that I won't pursue here. (What does "inner value" mean? What reason do we have to believe that whatever has an "inner value" is also "unconditional" and "raised above all price"?) But, whatever answer we give to these questions, one feature of Kant's moral theory stands out unmissably: its extraordinary combination of austerity and radicalism. Just one thing is said to have "unconditional, incomparable" value, and that turns out to be morality itself—the ultimate object of morality is morality! I shall return later to some of the implications that this idea has for the way that we should interpret Kant, but in this chapter my main concern is historical—how these thoughts of Kant's about dignity fit into the broader development of the understanding of dignity.

Central, as we have seen, is the idea, similar to Aquinas's, that whatever has dignity has an "unconditional, incomparable" value that is intrinsic to it. But we should also note the radical differences between the two thinkers. While Aquinas's idea sees dignity of different kinds, potentially at least, at all levels of God's creation (perhaps even including plants), Kant's conception is restricted to human beings. Only human beings (so far as we know) are capable of acting morally and feeling the force of morality's claims. For Pico della Mirandola (or Bacon or Pascal) the question of human dignity is the question: what *sort* of dignity do human beings have? The influence of Kant has helped make it natural for people now to assume that all dignity in the full sense of the word has to be *human* dignity. But before Kant this was not so—and nor was it so in the Catholic tradition after Kant. Kant's conception of dignity makes an exception of human beings from the rest of creation. Only morality has dignity and only human beings carry the moral law within themselves, so it would be wrong to think of human beings as part of the natural world in the way that rivers, trees, or dogs are. Yet Kant's conception of dignity is at the same time deeply egalitarian. Dignity is something that all human beings have in common. We are all (all of us who have attained the "age of reason," that is) subject to its demands, whatever place in society we may happen to occupy, and it is this that gives us our inalienable inner value.

Kant's view of dignity doesn't depend on God in the way that Aquinas's does. To attribute dignity to human beings, it is not necessary to make reference either to their creation in God's image or to their occupying an "appropriate" place within some divinely ordained natural hierarchy. Kant says (and I can see no reason to think that he did not mean this quite sincerely) that our moral nature comes from the fact that we have been created by God as free beings. But we can know that moral nature independently of any belief that we have in God, and it is this that founds our dignity. Nor do we need to see the natural world as subject to a divine will—human beings have dignity so long as they have morality, whatever external reality may turn out to be like. So Kant—whether he meant to do so or not—opened the way for a secular understanding of the dignity of human beings.

One aspect of Kant's conception of dignity that has a very modern sound is its connection with autonomy. Kant says that autonomy is "the ground of the dignity of human nature" (*Ak.* 4:436). It would seem, then, that those (like Macklin and Griffin mentioned earlier) who identify "dignity" with "autonomy" have Kant as their source. Looked at more closely, this is questionable, however. The word "autonomy" has two ingredients: *autos* (= "self") and (*nomos* = "law"). On an obvious understanding, being "a law unto oneself" means that the self is a sovereign, a kind of absolute monarch that can choose as it pleases. But this is very far from Kant's idea. Kant writes in the previous sentence that "the lawgiving itself, which determines all value, must for that very reason have a dignity" (*Ak.* 4:436)—it is, in the first instance, the "lawgiving" that has dignity. What Kant has in mind as *autonomy* is the idea that the moral law which we must acknowledge as binding upon us is "self-given." This is something quite different from the modern understanding of autonomy as the capacity of individuals to choose the course of their own lives however they see fit. But of course, whatever the proper interpretation of Kant's text may be, that does not mean that it has always been read in that way. At the very least Kant played a significant role in establishing the terminological link between dignity and autonomy.

Another feature that is still alive today is to be found in the same sentence. After asserting that lawgiving has a dignity, Kant continues: "and the word *respect* alone provides a becoming expression for the estimate of it that a rational being must give" (*Ak.* 4:436). By connecting dignity with respect, Kant is evidently relating dignity to its original sense as a status term—respect is the characteristic manner in which we acknowledge status—but he is doing it in a very distinctive, novel way. What is to be recognized as worthy of respect, according to Kant, is not the position that an individual occupies within a particular society, or even the generalized status of human beings as citizens of the world, but the lawgiving function of morality, something that human beings carry inalienably within themselves.

Outside the *Groundwork* Kant connects this essential, respect-worthy kernel of human agency with a wider account of our duties of respect. He discusses humility and self-respect in sections 11 and 12 of the "Doctrine of Virtue" in the *Metaphysics of Morals* (1797). Humility, he says, arises not from status comparison of ourselves with other individuals (which leads to the vice of servility) but by looking inward and comparing ourselves and our conduct with the demands made on us by the moral law. So, while the moral law should produce humility by bringing home to us the distance between who we are and who we ought to be, it should also inspire us with self-respect: "from our capacity for internal lawgiving and from the (natural) man feeling himself compelled to revere the (moral) man within his own person, at the same time there comes *exaltation* and the highest self-esteem, the feeling of his inner worth, . . . in terms of which he is above any price . . . and possesses an inalienable [*unverlierbare*] dignity . . . which instills in him respect for himself" (*Ak.* 6:436). Dignity is something that we all have in virtue of the "humanity in our person," and this founds duties of mutual respect and self-respect.

Self-respect, the form of pride in oneself that is proper to human beings, is a matter of *honor*—which is not to be confused with *arrogance*. "[Arrogance] differs from pride proper . . . which is *love of honor,* that is, a concern to yield nothing of one's human dignity in comparison with others (so that the adjective *'noble'* is usually added to 'pride' in this sense); for arrogance demands from others a respect it denies them" (*Ak.* 6:465). Honorable pride in ourselves requires that we demonstrate upright self-respect and independence even toward God: "Kneeling down or prostrating oneself on the ground, even to show your veneration for heavenly objects, is contrary to the dignity of humanity" (*Ak.* 6:436). In this way the Kantian idea of acknowledging the inherent dignity of morality underpins a strongly egalitarian—bourgeois, if you like—conception of honor as something that we owe to everyone (ourselves included) in equal measure, quite different from the aristocratic understanding of honor as part of a status hierarchy between inferiors and superiors.

Finally, I want to draw attention to a use of the term "dignity" in the *Groundwork* that carries a subtly—but significantly—different sense. At *Ak.* 4:439–440 (the fourteenth appearance of the term) Kant associates duty with "sublimity" *(Erhabenheit):*

> From what has just been said it is now easy to explain how it happens that, although in thinking the concept of duty we think of subjection to the law, yet at the same time we thereby represent a certain sublimity and *dignity* in the person who fulfills all his duties. For there is indeed no sublimity in him insofar as he is *subject* to the moral law, but there certainly is insofar as he is at the same time *lawgiving* with respect to it and only for that reason subordinated to it.

The sublime was a central category of eighteenth-century aesthetic theory, and Kant discusses it extensively in the *Critique of Judgement* (1790). Put simply, the sublime is something that, when we encounter it, goes beyond our comprehension and produces feelings of awe and wonder in us. Aesthetically, it is to be found, Kant says, "in a formless object insofar as *limitlessness* is represented in it" (*Ak.* 5:244). The connection between dignity and the sublime is not one that he makes in the *Critique of Judgement,* but it is easy enough to see. (Interestingly, Kant does associate the two ideas, although only in passing, in a much earlier work from 1764, *Observations on the Feeling of the Beautiful and the Sublime*.)

The German word *erhaben* means "superior" as well as being the conventional translation for "sublime." Thus, at *Ak.* 4:426, Kant describes the value of a thoroughly good will as *"erhaben"* above all price. The Cambridge translation—"raised above all price"—is certainly not wrong, but it misses the resonance of sublimity, which is unfortunate because, only two paragraphs earlier, Kant had referred to the "sublimity [*Erhabenheit*] and inner dignity of the command in a duty" (*Ak.* 4:425—the third use of dignity in the *Groundwork*). The moral law has unconditional value ("dignity" in Kant's use of the term, beyond "price") and it holds irrespective of any natural inclinations we might have. This transcendent quality, Kant asserts, should inspire awe and reverence in us in a way that is analogous to the awe-inspiring power of nature when it presents us with phenomena that go beyond our powers of perception. (The comparison brings to mind a very celebrated sentence from the conclusion to the *Critique of Practical Reason:* "Two things fill the mind with ever new and increasing wonder and reverence the more often and more steadily one reflects on them: the starry heavens above me and the moral law within me"; *Ak.* 5:161.)

What is notable about the passage at *Ak.* 4:439–440, however, is that in this case, unlike in the earlier passage, the "sublimity and dignity" referred to are not attributes of lawgiving or the moral law but qualities of character "in the person who fulfills all his duties." Rather than dignity being an intrinsic quality of all human beings insofar as they carry the moral law within themselves, it is a feature of those who follow the moral law's commands. This is only a very minor aspect of Kant's use of the term "dignity" (the passage at *Ak.* 4:439–440 is unique, so far as I know), but it is a significant one, for it connects the idea of dignity to a strand of its meaning that has so far remained in the background—dignity as a feature of behavior, the *dignified.* The possible connection between Kant's moral theory and the idea of dignity as a manifest quality of character or behavior is developed and explored by Friedrich Schiller in his essay *On Grace and Dignity* (1793).

But before moving on to Schiller, let me briefly bring together Kant's account. Most importantly, for Kant, to say that something has dignity is not to attribute a substantive value to it but to say that it has value of a particular kind—intrinsic, unconditional, and incomparable. Only one thing, however, actually has this intrinsic, unconditional, and incomparable value: morality, and humanity insofar as it is capable of morality. The dignity of the moral law makes human beings—its embodiment—worthy of respect. They should be respected by others and, equally importantly, they have the duty to respect themselves. The presence of the moral law in human beings has a double character: it makes human beings intrinsically valuable, while, at the same time, prescribing to them the way in which they should act. Since we are subject to the moral law and that law has its source within ourselves, human beings also embody "autonomy" (literally: their selves are the sources of law) and are thereby "raised above" the natural world. Hence, the dignity of the moral law is connected with the idea of it as something "sublime." Thus, Kant's is not a "naturalistic" theory (one that denies the specialness of human beings) but nor does our dignity depend on a religious perspective; we don't have to grasp the purposes of a creator-god to recognize it. Human beings have dignity because the moral law, the unique intrinsically and unconditionally valuable thing that there is, is embodied in us and in us alone, and this "inner transcendental kernel" is something that we all share equally. Under the influence of Kant, it has come to be taken for granted (outside the Catholic tradition, at least) that dignity is always human dignity and that dignity and equality go together.

IV. Grace and Dignity

"Dignity" as referring to what is dignified in manner was a commonly used category in the literature of criticism in the eighteenth century. (For instance, David Hume's relative and friend, Henry Home, Lord Kames's, book, *Elements of Criticism* [1762], contains a chapter called "Dignity and Grace," written very much in the style of Adam Smith's *Theory of the Moral Sentiments*.) Schiller's *On Grace and Dignity* (*Über Anmut und Würde,* 1793) can be seen as continuing that tradition. It is a wonderfully original work, however, in the way that it takes up these critical conceptions of grace and dignity and uses them to try to reconcile Kant's moral philosophy with the pagan ideal of the integration of mind and body, advocated by Schiller's friend Goethe.

Schiller gives a very succinct definition of "dignity" as an aesthetic quality. Dignity is, he writes, "tranquility in suffering." This conception of dignity is clearly derived from the great German art historian Johann Joachim Winckelmann (1717-1768). Winckelmann's impact on eighteenth-century German thought went far beyond aesthetics. His writings on classical art transformed the German perception of the ancient world and, through his influence on his many ardent disciples such as Herder and Goethe, established the image of Greece as the home of the harmonious integration of mind and body that was to be such a powerful force in German culture. In his first and most seminal work, *Thoughts on the Imitation of the Painting and Sculpture of the Greeks* (1755), Winckelmann includes an account of a famous work of classical sculpture, the *Laocoön* group. This sculpture once stood in the palace of Emperor Titus and had been praised in the highest terms by Pliny the Elder. Its rediscovery caused a sensation when it was unearthed in Rome in 1506. It depicts the death of the Trojan priest, Laocoön, and his sons. Laocoön, according to legend, had warned his fellow Trojans to beware of the Greeks' wooden horse, but the gods sent two serpents from the sea to strangle his sons, and Laocoön died in a vain attempt to save them. For Winckelmann, the key feature of the sculpture is the dignity with which Laocoön is depicted as enduring his suffering. As he writes,

> the universal and predominant characteristic
> of the Greek masterpieces is a noble simplicity
> and tranquil grandeur, both in posture and ex-
> pression. Just as the depths of the sea remain
> forever calm, however much the surface may

rage, so does the expression of the Greek figures, however strong their passions, reveal a great and dignified soul. Such a soul is depicted in the face of Laocoön, and not only in his face, despite his most violent torments. The pain which is evident in his every muscle and sinew, and which, disregarding his face and other parts of his body, we can almost feel ourselves simply by looking at his painfully contracted abdomen—this pain, I maintain, nevertheless causes no violent distortion either to his face or to his general posture. He raises no terrible clamour, as in Virgil's poetic account of his fate. His mouth is not wide enough open to allow it, and he emits instead an anxious and oppressed sigh, such as Sadoleto describes. The physical pain and spiritual greatness are diffused with equal intensity throughout his entire frame, and held, as it were, in balance. Laocoon suffers, but he suffers like the Philoctetes of Sophocles: his misery touches us to the heart, but we envy the fortitude with which the great man endures it.

Winckelmann's account of the Laocoön group had immense resonance among the educated public in Germany. Lessing's famous essay "Laocoön" was written in response to it, and the cast of the sculpture in the collection of the Elector Palatine in Mannheim became a destination of pilgrimage for German writers and artists (Herder, Goethe, and Schiller were among its many visitors).

For Schiller, grace and dignity are features of action or bearing. They figure in an account of human agency that (like Kant's) contrasts human beings' natural characters and desires—our "inclinations," in Kantian terminology— with the demands of morality that come from the rational, moral will *(der Wille).* Schiller was one of Kant's first readers (but by no means the last!) to be troubled by one apparent consequence of Kant's moral philosophy: according to Kant, a spontaneous, unreflective disposition to act well lacks any moral value (indeed, it may even be regarded as undesirable from a moral point of view). Against this, Schiller puts forward the idea of "grace." The graceful person is someone who does not just do the right thing but does it without any kind of internal struggle or painful process of choice. If our character is spontaneously in harmony with the requirements of morality, we are good without having to overcome any inner resistance.

The ideal of grace is not always achievable, however. Human beings have many inclinations that go against what would ideally be desirable from the moral point of view—selfishness, jealousy, and so on—and these need to be overcome. Some such conflicts will be there in even the best and noblest characters. Admirable characteristics like loyalty and affection for our friends and family, for example, can come into conflict with our duty to help to uphold the law when they have done wrong. When such a conflict opens up and the individual nevertheless shows the strength of character to overcome his or her inclinations and to act in the way required by morality, the characteristic manifestation of the action, says Schiller, is *dignity*. Dignity—here we can see the connection with Winckelmann—shows itself above all when we exercise self-control in the overcoming of suffering: "Just as grace is the expression of a beautiful soul, so dignity is the expression of a sublime disposition," Schiller writes, echoing and amplifying Kant's phrase about the "dignity and sublimity" of the person who fulfills all his duties. "Dignity and sublimity" belong to people who fulfill their duties while overcoming the force of their contrary inclinations. Their actions may not be "morally beautiful," he says, in the way that graceful ones are, but they are "morally great." Aesthetically, dignity functions as "the expression of the moral freedom of the human being"—it shows that we are not prisoners of our inclinations.

Schiller's innovative reinterpretation of dignity brings morality and aesthetics together and gives them a shared foundation in moral psychology. Grace and dignity are aesthetic qualities that arise as expressions of agency. Yet they are by no means separate from morality. They connect to the central feature of our moral situation as seen from the Kantian point of view: the permanent potential for conflict between our duties and our inclinations. Though it is closely connected to Kantian moral philosophy, Schiller's conception of dignity thus gives the term a new sense. Grace and dignity are the characteristic expressions of two cardinal moral virtues: the ability to act well spontaneously (grace) and the ability to act well despite the resistance of our natural inclinations (dignity). It follows that someone may have Schillerian dignity to a greater or lesser degree without lacking basic humanity. They will still have that unconditional and intrinsic moral value that comes from membership in the community of moral agents. Dignity is the commitment and capacity to endure suffering in the struggle to meet the demands of duty, and that obviously varies from person to person.

Reading Schiller's essay, one can see Kant's "bourgeois" conception of honor as the respect one owes to oneself as the embodiment of the moral law being complemented by a "bourgeois" conception of heroism and tragedy. True heroism is the willingness to endure suffering for the sake of moral duty. When the noble prisoner, Florestan, in Beethoven's opera *Fidelio* (1805), sings in his dungeon, *"Willig duld ich alle Schmerzen / Ende schmählich meine Bahn. / Süsse Trost in meinem Herzen / Meine Pflicht hab ich getan"* (I suffer all pains willingly, my way comes to a wretched end. A sweet consolation is in my heart: I have done my duty), he is showing a Schillerian kind of heroism. Such heroism is, in principle, available to everybody, not just those of "noble birth." All of us are subject to the moral law, and all of us—potentially, at least—may find ourselves called upon to sacrifice our well-being in the service of duty.

As is often the case with those who seek to reconcile warring parties in philosophy, Schiller's essay does not seem to have been appreciated by either side. In his lectures on moral philosophy (Vigilantius's transcript), Kant responds to Schiller by sharply re-asserting his doctrine regarding the necessity of the conflict between morality and "inclination":

> it is also certain that every obligation is forth-
> with associated with a moral constraint, and
> that it is contrary to the nature of duty to *enjoy*
> having duties incumbent on one; it is necessary,
> rather, that man's impulses should make him
> disinclined to fulfill the moral laws ... Assum-
> ing that man's fulfillment of the moral laws can
> be accomplished only under a necessitation, it
> cannot therefore be claimed, as Schiller does in
> his *Thalia* [the journal in which *On Grace and
> Dignity* was published] ... that such fulfillment
> also has a certain *grace* about it. (*Ak.* 27:490)

Interestingly, although Kant will have nothing to do
with Schiller's account of *grace* (the idea of a possible spontaneous harmony between duty and inclination), he is
not so hostile to the idea of *dignity* as the manifestation
of the struggle to overcome inclination. On the contrary,
in one of the many footnotes to the second edition of
Religion within the Limits of Reason Alone (1793, second edition 1794) Kant explains his disagreement with Schiller
by contrasting moral "grace" with his own account of the
dignity of morality:

> I readily grant that I am unable to associate
> *grace* with the *concept of duty,* by reason of duty's
> very dignity. For the concept of duty includes
> unconditional necessitation, to which grace-
> fulness stands in direct contradiction. The
> majesty of the law (like the law on Sinai) in-
> stills awe (not dread, which repels; and also not

> fascination, which invites familiarity); and this
> awe rouses the respect of the subject toward his
> master, except that in this case, since the mas-
> ter lies in us, it rouses a *feeling of the sublimity* of
> our own vocation that enraptures us more than
> any beauty. (*Ak.* 6:23)

As we have already seen, for Kant the dignity of the moral law (understood as an item of "unconditional, in-comparable" value, "raised above" any impulses from the senses) rouses a feeling of the sublime within human beings, and this is compatible with (if not quite the same as) Schiller's suggestion that human beings are *dignified* in character when their actions give expression to the struggle of duty to overcome the inclinations.

V. Dignity and Equality

Of course, at the very time that Kant and Schiller were writing, the entire system of social status in Europe was tottering from the impact of the French Revolution. The privileges (*dignités,* in French) of the aristocracy had been abolished and the idea of human beings as equal in rights and status asserted in their place. When that passionate opponent of the French Revolution, Hannah More (1745–1833) (in her day, an enormously popular evangelical pam-phleteer and a close ally of the anti-slavery campaigners Newton and Wilberforce) attacked contemporary appeals to the idea of human dignity, it is unlikely that it was two German philosophers, however eminent, whom she had in mind:

> We hear much and we hear falsely of the dig-
> nity of human nature. Prayer founded on the
> principles of Scripture alone teaches us wherein
> our true dignity consists. The dignity of a fallen
> creature is a perfect anomaly. True dignity,
> contrary to the common opinion that it is an
> inherent excellence, is actually a sense of the
> want of it; it consists not in our valuing our-
> selves but in a continual feeling of our depen-
> dence upon God and an unceasing aim at con-
> formity to his image.

So the idea of human dignity was very much a part of
the discourse of the time. An extremely interesting example of its use from the late eighteenth century comes
in the report of a famous, if unverified, conversation between John Bernard (an actor who traveled extensively in
America) and George Washington that took place in 1798.
Bernard met Washington when the two provided assis-
tance to a couple whose carriage had overturned. Afterward, Washington invited him to Mount Vernon. Bernard
describes an episode in their conversation:

> A black coming in at this moment, with a jug of
> spring water, I could not repress a smile, which
> the general at once interpreted. "This may seem
> a contradiction," he continued, "but I think
> you must perceive that it is neither a crime nor
> an absurdity. When we profess, as our funda-
> mental principle, that liberty is the inalienable
> right of every man, we do not include mad men
> or idiots; liberty in their hands would become a

scourge. Till the mind of the slave has been educated to perceive what are the obligations of a
state of freedom, and not confound a man's
with a brute's, the gift would insure its abuse.
We might as well be asked to pull down our
old warehouses before trade has increased to de-
mand enlarged new ones. Both houses and slaves
were bequeathed to us by Europeans, and time
alone can change them; an event, sir, which,
you may believe me, no man desires more heart-
ily than I do. Not only do I pray for it, on *the
score of human dignity,* but I can clearly foresee
that nothing but the rooting out of slavery can
perpetuate the existence of our union, by con-
solidating it in a common bond of principle."
(my emphasis)

Whatever the reliability of Bernard's account of Washington's views on slavery (what a convenient piece of pre-
science, you might think, for "the father of the nation" to
be shown darkly foreseeing the threat to the Union from
the evil of slavery in a memoir published after the Civil
War), the use of the language of human dignity here is
still striking. It confirms, surely, that a simultaneous
tendency toward equality was making itself felt in each
of the three different strands of the meaning of dignity—
dignity as status, dignity as intrinsic value, and dignity as
dignified manner or bearing—that we have distinguished
so far. The French Revolution embodied a strongly egalitarian political interpretation of the status idea of dig-

nity. It revived the Ciceronian conception of dignity as a matter of the status of human beings as such (rather than a person's relative position in any particular society), which, in turn, made it natural to represent slavery as a violation of human dignity. At the same time, Kant and Schiller had reached an egalitarian conception of dignity by their own route. For Kant, the idea of dignity as intrinsic value was to be identified with a feature that all (and only) human beings have in common, while Schiller moralized the idea of dignified behavior into something potentially achievable by all human beings, since all of us alike face the possibility of conflicts between duty and inclination.

Thus, although I think that Schopenhauer exaggerates how far the nineteenth-century idea of human dignity derived from Kant, it seems plausible to think that, by the time that he was writing (1839), the various strands of "human dignity" had indeed become fused into a cliché of pious humanitarianism. Nor is it surprising to find "dignity" opposed by liberalism's contemporary critics. It was not just Schopenhauer who reacted against the pervasiveness of appeals to human dignity. Marx denounces another German socialist, Karl Heinzen, for describing the rule of the German princes as contrary to the "dignity of man." Such "empty phrases" about dignity amount to "[taking] refuge from history in morality," Marx alleges.

But the most vehement nineteenth-century attack on the idea of dignity that I have come across is to be found in a little-known essay by Nietzsche. The essay, which has the title "The Greek State," was one of the *Five Prefaces to*

Five Unwritten Books, given to Cosima Wagner as a birthday present in 1872 (the year of the publication of *The Birth of Tragedy*). It opens as follows:

> We moderns have an advantage over the Greeks in two ideas, which are given as it were as a compensation to a world behaving thoroughly slavishly and yet at the same time anxiously eschewing the word "slave": we talk of the "dignity of man" and of the "dignity of labour." Everybody worries in order miserably to perpetuate a miserable existence; this awful need compels man to consuming labour; he (or, more exactly, the human intellect) seduced by the "will" now occasionally marvels at labour as something dignified. However, in order that labour might have a claim on titles of honor, it would be necessary above all, that existence itself, to which labour after all is only a painful means, should have more dignity and value than it appears to have had, up to the present, to serious philosophies and religions.

The idea of the dignity of labor, says Nietzsche, is a way of trying to make more attractive what is in fact a shameful necessity as a consolation for those who are forced to undertake it. This, however, is to give both labor and human existence itself (for which labor is the necessary precondition) a value that they do not deserve. The Greeks, on the other hand, according to Nietzsche, "did not require such conceptual hallucinations . . . for among them the idea that labour is a disgrace is expressed with startling frankness." It is only the humanitarianism of the nineteenth century that requires such sentimental fictions:

> Such phantoms as the dignity of man, the dignity of labour, are the needy products of slavedom hiding itself from itself. Woeful time, in which the slave requires such conceptions, in which he is incited to think about and beyond himself! Cursed seducers, who have destroyed the slave's state of innocence by the fruit of the tree of knowledge! Now the slave must vainly scrape through from one day to another with transparent lies recognizable to every one of deeper insight, such as the alleged "equal rights of all" or the so-called "fundamental rights of man," of man as such, or the "dignity of labour."

Nietzsche himself actually invokes the concept of dignity, but he does it in a way that is diametrically opposed to the egalitarianism behind rights-based conceptions of human dignity. The slave, says Nietzsche, cannot

> understand at what stage and at what height dignity can first be mentioned, namely, at the point, where the individual goes wholly beyond himself and no longer has to work and to produce in order to preserve his individual existence.

Existence as such has no value. The only thing that can give value to life is culture—art—and for that, leisure (and, hence, slavish labor on behalf of those who are to have that leisure) is necessary. Existence is redeemed by culture; culture requires labor; labor is subordination; therefore, slavery is justified because it is necessary to what is intrinsically valuable, the life of the free, creative aristocrat:

> Accordingly we must accept this cruel sounding [only "sounding," Friedrich?] truth, *that slavery is of the essence of culture;* a truth of course, which leaves no doubt as to the absolute value of existence. This truth is the vulture, that gnaws at the liver of the Promethean promoter of Culture. The misery of toiling men must still increase in order to make the production of the world of art possible to a small number of Olympian men ... Therefore we may compare this grand Culture with a blood-stained victor, who in his triumphal procession carries the defeated along as slaves chained to his chariot, slaves whom a beneficent power has so blinded that, almost crushed by the wheels of the chariot, they nevertheless still exclaim: "Dignity of labour!" "Dignity of Man!"

Sentimental egalitarianism pervades the modern state and leads, according to Nietzsche, not just to such hypocritical and absurd ideas as the dignity of labor and the dignity of man but to a more general humanitarianism that shows itself in a fear of war. Nietzsche has no such scruples (he is writing, of course, just after the Franco-Prussian war, in which he participated with great enthusiasm). Nietzsche contrasts the modern state with the warrior-state of the ancient Greeks. Such a form of social organization is, says Nietzsche, the "prototype of the state." The fact that the whole state was organized on the basis of the most efficient military structure produced "an immediate decomposition and division of the chaotic mass into *military castes,* out of which rises, pyramid-shaped, on an exceedingly broad base of slaves, the edifice of 'martial society.'" The characteristic of such a structure is the complete subordination of those in the lower orders to those higher on the pyramid. Not that this hierarchy is inimical to dignity as Nietzsche understands it—as he lets us know in no uncertain terms as he stands humanism on its head in his peroration:

> If we now imagine the military primal state in its greatest activity, at its proper "labour," and if we fix our glance upon the whole technique of war, we cannot avoid correcting our notions picked up from everywhere, as to the "dignity of man" and the "dignity of labour" by the question, whether the idea of dignity is applicable also to that labour, which has as its purpose the destruction of the "dignified" man, as well as to the man who is entrusted with that "dignified labour," or whether in this warlike

task of the state those mutually contradictory ideas do not neutralize one another. I should like to think the warlike man to be a *means* of the military genius and his labour again only a tool in the hands of that same genius; and not to him, as absolute man and non-genius, but to him as a means of the genius—whose pleasure also can be to choose his tool's destruction as a mere pawn sacrificed on the strategist's chess-board—is due a degree of dignity, of that dignity namely, *to have been deemed worthy of being a means of the genius.* But what is shown here in a single instance is valid in the most general sense; every human being, with his total activity, only has dignity in so far as he is a tool of the genius, consciously or unconsciously; from this we may immediately deduce the ethical conclusion, that "man in himself," the absolute man possesses neither dignity, nor rights, nor duties; only as a wholly determined being serving unconscious purposes can man excuse his existence.

Nietzsche's extraordinary polemic sets in relief how far the concept of dignity had developed in his day into an amalgam of humanist, liberal, Christian, socialist, and Kantian ideas—all of which Nietzsche loathed, of course, with more or less equal intensity.

VI. Hierarchy

We might think, then, that this nineteenth-century egal-itarian convergence around the various senses of dignity established the ground for the assertions of universal human dignity that we find in the major post–Second World War human rights documents, the Universal Dec-laration and the German Grundgesetz. But this would be a very significant mistake. It would oversimplify the story and so miss the roots of some of the significant tensions and conflicts that we find in modern uses of the term.

For one thing, the use of the term "dignity" to denote the bearing required by a differentiated status hierarchy had not disappeared. It is no surprise to find De Toc-queville, whose aristocratic worldview is so apparent on every page he writes, using dignity in this sense in *Democracy in America:*

> True dignity in manners consists in always tak-ing one's proper station, neither too high nor too low, and this is as much within the reach of a peasant as of a prince. In democracies all stations appear doubtful; hence it is that the manners of democracies, though often full of arrogance, are commonly wanting in dignity, and, moreover, they are never either well trained or accomplished. (vol. 2, pt. 3, chap. 14)

The Aquinian conception of "dignity" as the value something has in virtue of occupying its proper place within a divine order also remained central to nineteenth-century Catholic thought.

Pope Leo XIII (1810–1903) is best known today outside the Catholic Church for his encyclical on the relationship between labor and capital, *Rerum Novarum* of 1891, which established the idea of the "dignity of labor" within the Catholic tradition. The idea of the "dignity of labor" had already been advanced by many liberals and socialists, but we would be quite wrong to infer from this that Leo's advocacy of the dignity of labor expressed his endorsement of social egalitarianism. Here to illustrate the place of dignity in Leo's social views is an extract from his encyclical *Quod Apostolici Muneris* of 1878:

> For, He who created and governs all things has, in His wise providence, appointed that the things which are lowest should attain their ends by those which are intermediate, and these again by the highest. Thus, as even in the kingdom of heaven He hath willed that the choirs of angels be distinct and some subject to others, and also in the Church has instituted various orders and a diversity of offices, so that all are not apostles or doctors or pastors, so also has He appointed that there should be various orders in civil society, *differing in dignity, rights, and power, whereby the State, like the Church, should be one body, consisting of many members, some nobler than others, but all necessary to each other and solicitous for the common good.* (6, my emphasis)

For the Catholic Church in the nineteenth century, all members of society have dignity, but their dignity consists in their playing the role that is appropriate to their station within a hierarchical social order, one in which some are "nobler than others." Instead of sharing in equal dignity, the orders of society should differ in "dignity, rights and power." Leo's defense of the propriety of hierarchy does not stop at the front door. In *Arcanum divinae sapientiae* (1880), he asserts the inequality of men and women in marriage:

> The woman, because she is flesh of his flesh and bone of his bone, must be subject to her husband and obey him; [an invalid inference from a false premise if ever I saw one!] not, indeed, as a servant, but as a companion, so that her obedience shall be wanting in neither honour nor dignity. (11)

Note that "dignity" here is not an attribute of an individual person—the wife—but is applied to an aspect of a social relationship in which she finds herself, "her obedience." The use of "dignity" here ascribes value to the subordination itself. Seen in this context, the idea of the "dignity of labor," as introduced into the social teaching of the Church by Leo, should be understood less as an assertion of equality than an expression of the view that labor should be given its proper place within a social order, all of whose members are "necessary to each other, and solicitous of the common good."

In the 1881 encyclical *Diuturnum* (On the Origin of Civil Power), Leo expresses his outrage at the degree to which in modern society "pains have been taken to render rulers the object of contempt and hatred to the multitude." The "flames of envy," as he calls them, have "burst forth" and put "the security of rulers ... in peril" (2, 3). For this Leo blames egalitarian theories of popular sovereignty and the social contract:

> Very many men of more recent times ... say that all power comes from the people; so that those who exercise it in the State do so not as their own, but as delegated to them by the people, and that, by this rule, it can be revoked by the will of the very people by whom it was delegated. But from these, Catholics dissent, who affirm that the right to rule is from God, as from a natural and necessary principle. (5)

Only once false views of popular sovereignty have been rejected, and an understanding of government as incorporating the transmission of divine authority from ruler to ruled has been restored, will government have its proper dignity:

> It is plain, moreover, that the pact which they allege is openly a falsehood and a fiction, and that it has no authority to confer on political power such great force, dignity, and firmness as the safety of the State and the common good of the citizens require. Then only will the govern-

ment have all those ornaments and guarantees,
when it is understood to emanate from God as
its august and most sacred source. (12)

Leo's animus against the idea of popular sovereignty
is typical of Catholic thought of his time. It is largely forgotten nowadays how far the Catholic Church throughout the nineteenth century and well into the twentieth
was engaged in a rearguard action against egalitarianism
in its various forms: liberalism, socialism, democracy,
and the emancipation of women. (Two of the relatively
few constitutions to incorporate the term "dignity" prior
to 1948 were Salazar's Portugal and Franco's Spain—both
Catholic countries and neither of them exactly paradises
of social equality and respect for human rights.) It is important to recognize the anti-egalitarian character of so
much Catholic thought about dignity in order to appreciate just how great the change was that took place in
Catholic social thought around the middle of the twentieth century. In taking for granted that there is an inherent
connection between the idea of human dignity and equal
human rights—as it would be easy to do if we look at such
documents as the Universal Declaration and the Grund-
esetz without a historical perspective—we miss what a
significant event the Catholic acceptance of the doctrine
of social equality has been.

Nowadays the Catholic Church pursues its fight against
secular conceptions of human dignity in socially egalitarian terms. Thus in *Evangelium Vitae* (1995), John Paul II
argues that there is a contradiction between "the various

declarations of human rights and the many initiatives inspired by these declarations [which] show that at the global level there is a growing moral sensitivity, more alert to acknowledging the value and dignity of every individual as a human being, without any distinction of race, nationality, religion, political opinion or social class" (18) and (as he takes it) the unjust denial of equal rights in liberal-democratic societies to the unborn and to those in persistent vegetative states.

Likewise, in his apostolic letter *Mulieris Dignitatem* (1988), John Paul II rejects the idea that women should be subservient to men. This, he says (in striking contrast to Leo XIII), is contrary to women's rights. Yet at the same time he asserts strongly that the dignity of the "specific diversity and personal originality" of the two sexes must be maintained:

> In our times the question of "women's rights" has taken on new significance in the broad context of the rights of the human person. The biblical and evangelical message sheds light on this cause, which is the object of much attention today, by safeguarding the truth about the "unity" of the "two," that is to say the truth about that dignity and vocation that result from the specific diversity and personal originality of man and woman. Consequently, even the rightful opposition of women to what is expressed in the biblical words "He shall rule over you" (Gen. 3:16) must not under any condi-

tion lead to the "masculinization" of women. In the name of liberation from male "domination," women must not appropriate to themselves male characteristics contrary to their own feminine "originality." There is a well-founded fear that if they take this path, women will not "reach fulfilment," but instead will deform and lose what constitutes their essential richness. (10)

At what point did Catholicism lose its ambivalence about liberalism and democracy and accept the idea of human dignity as entailing social and political equality? It is very hard to say for sure, not least because an organization whose public stance claims that its teaching embodies the authority of scriptural revelation and timeless natural law is obviously reluctant to admit that it has changed its mind. My own belief is that the Second World War was a watershed. Certainly, Catholic influence on the Universal Declaration of Human Rights (particularly through the Catholic thinker Jacques Maritain) and the German Grundgesetz was crucial, in ensuring both that dignity was given such a prominent place and that it was connected with the idea of inviolable human rights.

The contrast between dignity and equal human rights is still alive elsewhere, however. This is evident enough in the Cairo Declaration on Human Rights in Islam (issued in 1990 by the Organization of the Islamic Conference), whose Article 6 asserts that women have "equal dignity"—but not (and here it is in conspicuous and unquestionably conscious contrast to the Universal Declaration) *equal rights.*

VII. Respect for Rights and the Right to Respect

So where does this leave us?

I started by pointing out that the idea of dignity is invoked in the Universal Declaration and the Grundgesetz in connection with human rights—human beings are "free and equal in dignity and rights" or they have "inviolable" dignity and (therefore) "inviolable and inalienable" rights. Human rights are obviously deeply puzzling—almost everyone nowadays professes commitment to them, yet few people would claim that they had a good, principled account of what they are and why we have them. Could a modern understanding of dignity meet that need? If it did, it would, ideally, have to do three things. First, it would explain and justify the claim that all human beings share "inviolable" dignity and that they are "free and equal" in that dignity. Second, it would show that it followed from this that they also have inviolable and inalienable rights. Third and finally, it would identify what those rights were. Can the account of dignity that we have given so far satisfy such an agenda?

The answer, presumably, will be different depending on which of the three strands of meaning of dignity distinguished up till now—the idea of dignity as status, the idea of dignity as inherent value, and the idea of dignity as behavior, character, or bearing that is dignified—one focuses on. If the idea of dignity is that of status, then to say that human beings are born "free and equal" in dignity is simply to assert that there are no intrinsic status differences between them. The idea that we are all equal in social status was not always the commonplace that it is nowadays (think only of Leo XIII and the hierarchical tradition of Catholic social teaching), but to say that human beings have equal dignity in this sense doesn't give a foundation to the claim that they have equal rights: it just assumes it. Looking at dignity as inherent value and interpreting that as some kind of inner transcendental kernel seems more promising. Kant maintains that we have dignity in the sense of "unconditional, incomparable value" because we—all of us, equally—contain within ourselves the moral law to which we are subject. Does that lead to the possession of rights? Kant certainly thinks so. For the Kantian, the prime feature of morality is the duty it requires of us unconditionally. But fundamental among those duties is respect for the rights of others. In one of the transcripts of his lectures on ethics, Kant gives a vivid and eloquent account of the centrality of rights to his conception of morality:

> [Duties towards others of indebtedness and justice] rest upon the universal rule of right, and the supreme duty of them all is respect for the rights of others. They are impregnable and inviolable. Woe unto him who infringes those rights, and tramples them underfoot! The right of the other should keep him secure in everything; it is stronger than any bulwark or wall.

> We have a divine ruler, and his sacred gift to us
> is the rights of man. (*Ak.* 27:415)

Yet not only (as we shall see) is it controversial what
rights the Kantian conception of human dignity entails, we are, it hardly needs to be said, not all Kantians.
To take an obvious example, the Catholic tradition of
thought about dignity as intrinsic value, which played
such an important role in the human rights documents
of the immediate post-war years, is very different from
the Kantian one. The German Grundgesetz represents an
ambitious—yes, you could even say, heroic—attempt to
turn the Kantian and Catholic conceptions of human dignity into a shared, articulated account of human rights.
The difficulties that it faces (some of which will be discussed in Chapter 2) are, I think, instructive in helping
us understand the strengths and weaknesses of the Kantian view.

Finally, we had the understanding of dignity as what is
"dignified." It might seem obvious from what has been
said earlier that dignity in this sense is extraneous to
what is at issue in the Universal Declaration and the
Grundgesetz. In Schiller's hands, the conception of dignity as what is dignified is part of an account of morally
admirable behavior—dignity in this sense is an expression of steadfastness of purpose and tranquility in suffering. But of course, human rights are for everyone, not
just for virtuous heroes; we don't lose our rights if we
behave less than ideally. Yet, surprisingly perhaps, this
understanding of dignity is by no means irrelevant for
understanding the role that dignity now plays in human

rights discourse, and I'd like to bring this chapter to a close by adding as a fourth strand a way in which the idea of dignity as the dignified should figure within the comprehension of dignity.

To introduce it, let me return to Joel Feinberg's thought about the connection between human dignity and respect for the rights of persons: "Respect for persons may simply be respect for their rights, so that there cannot be one without the other; and what is called 'human dignity' may simply be the recognizable capacity to assert claims. To respect a person, then, or to think of him as possessed of human dignity simply is to think of him as a potential maker of claims." Just as I respect the speed limit by driving below a certain speed, I respect rights by not infringing them (if they are negative) or doing what they require if they are positive. Let me call respect in this sense "respect-as-observance." If Feinberg is right and "respect-as-observance" is what respecting human dignity involves, then invoking the duty to respect human dignity doesn't identify or justify human rights; in fact, it presupposes their existence. Without first knowing the content of those rights we could not know how to respect dignity, any more than we could observe the law without knowing that there was a speed limit.

The dignified person, on the other hand, is someone who *shows* dignity in their character or bearing. To follow Schiller, it is a manifestation of a moral capacity—the ability to resist natural impulses. Calling a football manager "dignified" and "stoical" in the face of rudeness and unfair criticism makes sense because he resisted the impulse to lose emotional self-control and respond angrily or in other ways to manifest the natural effects of being treated in a humiliating way. But if being dignified is something that one shows, is there not a corresponding idea about the way one should be treated—the right to be treated *with dignity?* To treat someone *with dignity* is (it seems natural to say) to *respect* their dignity. But this is "respect" in a sense that is different from "respect-as-observance." Let me call it "respect-as-respectfulness." To respect someone's dignity by treating them with dignity requires that one *shows* them respect, either positively, by acting toward them in a way that gives expression to one's respect, or, at least, negatively, by refraining from behavior that would show disrespect.

In this context another of the founding documents of post-war human rights practice, the Geneva Conventions of 1949, is extremely illuminating. Article 3 of Convention III (the convention relative to the treatment of prisoners of war) reads as follows:

> Art 3. In the case of armed conflict not of an international character occurring in the territory of one of the High Contracting Parties, each Party to the conflict shall be bound to apply, as a minimum, the following provisions:
>
> (1) Persons taking no active part in the hostilities, including members of armed forces who have laid down their arms and those placed hors de combat by sickness, wounds, detention, or any other cause, shall in all circumstances be

treated humanely, without any adverse distinction founded on race, colour, religion or faith, sex, birth or wealth, or any other similar criteria. To this end the following acts are and shall remain prohibited at any time and in any place whatsoever with respect to the above-mentioned persons:

(a) *violence to life and person, in particular murder of all kinds, mutilation, cruel treatment and torture;*

(b) taking of hostages;

(c) *outrages upon personal dignity, in particular, humiliating and degrading treatment;*

(d) the passing of sentences and the carrying out of executions without previous judgment pronounced by a regularly constituted court affording all the judicial guarantees which are recognized as indispensable by civilized peoples.

(2) The wounded and sick shall be collected and cared for.

An impartial humanitarian body, such as the International Committee of the Red Cross, may offer its services to the Parties to the conflict. (my emphasis)

Here we have a document that is contemporary with the Universal Declaration and the Grundgesetz, but one that gives a significantly different content to "dignity." Where the former made dignity something that is (presumably) foundational to basic human rights in general, there is a clear separation in the Geneva Convention, as we can see in the contrast between clauses 1(a) and 1(c), between dignity and other human rights. Violence to life and person (murder, cruel treatment, and torture) are outlawed in clause 1(a), while violations of dignity, exemplified by humiliating and degrading treatment, are prohibited in a separate clause, 1(c). I think it is clear from this that what is at issue in the Geneva Convention is dignity, not in the sense of providing the foundation for some basic set of human rights (which are addressed in the earlier clause), but dignity in the sense of a requirement that people (in this case, prisoners of war) should be treated respectfully—that they have a right to be treated "with dignity." In this way, the Geneva Conventions present a different sense of dignity from the Universal Declaration and the Grundgesetz.

Such a right to dignified treatment is potentially a universal right. If we think of dignity as the achievement of someone who has managed to overcome resistance to act in a dignified way, not everyone will be dignified. Nevertheless, it is perfectly coherent to claim that everyone—even those of us who don't have the moral strength to behave in a dignified way when we are faced with moral challenges—should be treated "with dignity." They should be treated "with respect"—that is, most importantly, they should not be treated disrespectfully by being humiliated or degraded. Dignity, understood as being treated with respect in this way, connects back to an idea that we encountered in the discussion of Kant. Although, for Kant, dignity is the inherent value that the moral law within us has, the fact that we are the embodied bearers of this moral law forms the basis of a duty of respect that we owe both to other people and ourselves. Perhaps a part of this is "respect-as-observance" (we should respect the rights that people have in virtue of being bearers of the moral law), but it is also "respect-as-respectfulness." We must respect the dignity of the moral law within us by behaving in ways that express our respect for it—by our upright bearing and proper pride in ourselves, for example.

To sum up, we have seen that the idea of dignity as intrinsic value played a very important role in the founding documents of modern human rights discourse, but that there are at least two very different ways of understanding what it means there—the Kantian and the Catholic. The assertion of human dignity as a status human beings have, not because of their position within a particular society but simply because of their common humanity, may have had a very significant critical role in denying the legitimacy of hierarchies based on social stratification, yet it does not seem capable of playing a constructive role in helping us to identify a specific bundle of human rights as fundamental. Finally, the third strand examined, the idea of dignity as behavior that is dignified, reveals a fourth: a perspective on dignity from which to treat someone *with dignity* is to treat them with respect. Instead of respecting dignity by respecting a set of fundamental rights, dignity requires respectfulness. Taken in this way, the right to have one's dignity respected is one particular right—albeit a very important one—rather than something that acts as the foundation for rights in general.

2

THE LEGISLATION OF DIGNITY

I. Dwarves with Dignity

In October 1995 the Conseil d'État (the court of highest instance for French administrative law) adjudicated a case brought by a M. Manuel Wackenheim against the commune of Morsang-sur-Orge. On October 25, 1991, the Mayor of Morsang-sur-Orge had issued an order banning a dwarf-tossing competition due to take place at a local discotheque. M. Wackenheim, a dwarf, wearing a protective suit, was to be thrown by the competitors, landing on a suitably placed airbed. The Mayor banned the planned competition using his police powers for the maintenance of public order and safety. M. Wackenheim appealed against this ban and, in a ruling of February 1992, the Administrative Court in Versailles annulled the Mayor's order on the following grounds:

> The evidence on file does not show that the banned event was of a nature to disturb public order, peace or health in the town of Morsang-sur-Orge; the mere fact that certain notable

individuals may have voiced public disapproval of such an event being held could not be taken to suggest that a disturbance of public order might ensue; even supposing, as the mayor maintains, that the event might have represented a degrading affront to human dignity, a ban could not be legally ordered in the absence of particular local circumstances.

It was this ruling that was now before the Conseil d'État. As the judgment of the Conseil d'État explains, the police powers given to municipalities for the control of public entertainments were primarily intended to guarantee the safety of the public and to prevent possible material infractions of public order. But in this case the Mayor had forbidden the dwarf-tossing contest because, in his opinion, such entertainments represented a "violation of respect for the dignity of the human person." Traditionally, the notion of "public order," in the name of which the Mayor's police powers were being exercised, had been interpreted in French law as covering three aspects: security, peacefulness, and public health. However, there existed past cases in which aspects of public morality had been included within the notion of public order used to justify the exercise of public police powers—for example, in closing brothels, regulating the costumes of bathers on public beaches, imposing standards on the inscriptions on gravestones in public cemeteries, and the naming of public highways. The Conseil d'État took the view that the protection of dignity was another example of the acceptable inclusion of public morality within the definition of "public order." Accordingly, it ruled that the Mayor of Morsang was acting within his powers and the decision of the Administrative Court was reversed. On its website, the Conseil d État gave the following analysis of its decision:

> In deciding the case in question, the court of appeal was of the opinion that the entertainment of "dwarf throwing," consisting of the throwing of a dwarf by members of the public, leads to using a person affected by a physical handicap and presented as such as a projectile. An attraction of this sort was regarded as infringing the dignity of the human person in its very objective. Its prohibition was thus legal, even in the absence of particular local circumstances.
>
> In ascribing to the municipal authorities exercising police powers the power to forbid public entertainments disturbing to the conscience because infringing the dignity of the human person, the Conseil d'État has shown that public order could not be defined in a purely "material and external" manner, but included a conception of human beings for which public authorities must require the proper respect.

M. Wackenheim, however, was obviously a person of considerable determination. Having been defeated in the highest court of his own country, he took things further and appealed to the Human Rights Committee of the United Nations, established under the International Covenant on Civil and Political Rights (1966), to which France is a signatory. France was also a signatory to the "Optional Protocol" to the Covenant, which, as I understand it, allows individuals the right of direct appeal to the Human Rights Committee. It was this right that M. Wackenheim exercised. M. Wackenheim, by the way, had, apparently, already complained to the European Commission on Human Rights, which rejected his appeal in October 1996. Interestingly, the concept of dignity *does not* appear in the European Convention on Human Rights. M. Wackenheim appealed under Article 5 (the right to liberty and security of persons), Article 8 (the right to respect for private and family life), and Article 14 (the right to non-discrimination).

In July 2002 the UN Human Rights Committee too rejected M. Wackenheim's claim. Although M. Wackenheim and his counsel maintained that the prohibition of dwarf throwing, so far from protecting M. Wackenheim's dignity, actually violated it, by preventing him from taking up employment of his own choice, the UN Human Rights Committee did not address this issue. The International Covenant on Civil and Political Rights (unlike the UN Declaration of Human Rights, to which it was intended to give institutional weight) does not mention the protection of human dignity or the right to choose one's employment. Thus the Committee decided that only one of M. Wackenheim's complaints fell within their purview, namely, his complaint under Article 26 of the Covenant, prohibiting discrimination. Since, as the Committee pointed out, not all differentiation between persons constitutes (objectionable) discrimination, the issue before the Committee was whether M. Wackenheim's treatment was based on "objective and reasonable grounds." In the Committee's opinion, it was:

> If these persons [dwarves] are covered to the exclusion of others, the reason is that they are the only persons capable of being thrown. Thus, the differentiation between the persons covered by the ban, namely dwarves, and those to whom it does not apply, namely persons not suffering from dwarfism, is based on an objective reason and is not discriminatory in its purpose. The Committee considers that the State party has demonstrated, in the present case, that the ban on dwarf throwing as practised by the author did not constitute an abusive measure but was necessary in order to protect public order, which brings into play considerations of human dignity that are compatible with the objectives of the Covenant.

And at this point, so far as I can tell, M. Wackenheim's long march through the institutions of the law came to an end. I have followed his progress in some detail not (just) out of sympathy with him but because of the light that it gives on the place of dignity in contemporary jurisprudence. In my opinion, M. Wackenheim's case shows that the ubiquity of dignity in current legal discourse masks a great deal of disagreement and sheer confusion.

I can't help thinking that M. Wackenheim got a pretty raw deal. The Mayor of Morsang-sur-Orge justified his original intervention in the name of the protection of "the dignity of the human person," a claim that was maintained all the way to the UN Human Rights Committee. On the other hand, M. Wackenheim's claim that his own dignity was being infringed by not being allowed to take up the employment of his choice (or, as he might equally well have argued, to behave as he pleased in a place that was public only in the sense of being attended by a considerable number of paying customers, not in the sense that anyone might inadvertently have stumbled upon what went on there and been offended by it) carried no force. It may be (I am no lawyer) that he was unfortunate, inasmuch as the conventions under which he appealed (the International Covenant on Civil and Political Rights, the European Convention on Human Rights) make no explicit mention of dignity. However, a great deal of contemporary dignity jurisprudence *infers* the concept of dignity, rather than relying on its explicit mention in statute or convention. Moreover, the International Covenant was developed as a means of implementing the Universal Declaration of Human Rights, where dignity is indeed explicit.

There can be no argument, in my opinion, but that dwarf-tossing is undignified. But then again so are many other human activities. To judge by my experience, if the state takes it upon itself to prevent undignified behavior in clubs and bars late at night, it will, to say the least, have its work cut out for it! And should it even try to do so? First of all, who is harmed by undignified behavior? If it is the person who behaves in an undignified way, then, if he or she does so willingly and in full awareness of the consequences (I don't think that anyone could doubt this about M. Wackenheim, given how much trouble he went to fighting his case!), what business is it of the state to stop them? Doesn't being treated with dignity mean that we should have the right to make our own choices about whether to behave with dignity or not? Does the state's duty to protect "the dignity of the human person" entail that it has the right to prohibit people from choosing to behave in an undignified way? Perhaps my behaving in an undignified way is not a particularly good use of my power of choice, but should I not still be allowed to choose to do so?

Now you might object to what I have just said that it is not just a matter of requiring dwarves to behave in a dignified way to protect some inner transcendental kernel that they carry within themselves—"the dignity of the human person." As a matter of fact, there are people (other than M. Wackenheim himself) whom dwarf-tossing harms, namely, the community of dwarves. When the issue of dwarf-tossing arose in America, it was vigorously opposed by the organization Little People of America on the grounds that dwarf-tossing "tears down the structure and the esteem that little people are trying to gain." A similar argument is often made against prostitution. Yes, it is said, it might be (although, in fact, it rarely is) that prostitutes sell their sexual services in a wholly voluntary, uncoerced, unexploited way. But even then, what they do damages other women. Men paying women for sex undermines (to put it briefly) the nature of the sexual relationship between men and women even in other cases where there is no question of money changing hands.

To this, however, there are some quick replies to be made. Just because someone acts in a way that has the effect of lowering esteem for you doesn't mean that you have the right to have their behavior prohibited. Imagine, for example, that a group of school students behaves in a way that damages the esteem for the rest of their class. Let's assume that this behavior isn't something that would be legally prohibited in itself—they aren't going around breaking windows or anything like that—but just, say, getting a reputation for laziness and rudeness. Perhaps in this case their fellow students would have a right to complain to them about their behavior, but do they have the right to have it banned? I surely hope not. The trouble is that the word "dignity" carries the absolutist resonance that comes from its association with the idea of an inner transcendental kernel of inalienable value. If someone were to violate *that,* of course, it would be a serious matter and the state shouldn't stand idly by. But being esteemed less because one happens to be associated in others' minds with the behavior of someone who behaves in an undignified way? I'm sorry, but in my view people just have to put up with it.

You may also think that giving someone the right to behave in an undignified way isn't an important right for them to have. Being undignified, I imagine you objecting, is a bad thing for the person concerned, and though we have good reasons to let people to do things that are bad for them that only harm themselves (like smoking or eating unhealthy food), those reasons are chiefly because we don't want an interfering state to treat people as if it were a nanny. Once other people are harmed by such behavior as well, it's a different matter, surely.

At this point I want to ask, though: is being undignified always a bad thing? Might the abandonment of dignity not, in fact, be something that (in the right circumstances) is very valuable—both for the person who behaves in an undignified way and for other people? When I ask you to think of someone as "dignified," what sort of an image comes to mind? My guess is that it is someone older (rather than younger), quite probably grey-haired, tall (rather than short), soberly dressed—perhaps in a robe (not, like Laocoön, in a loincloth), slow-moving, powerful (rather than agile), and, almost certainly, male. And if I were to ask you to give me an example of someone who was "worthy," I think that you might (particularly if you are a British native speaker of English) think of an old-style "civic dignitary"—an alderman, perhaps.

With that in mind, here is an extract from a story about the opening of the Haggerston Baths in the "go-ahead borough" of Shoreditch ("which regard[s] public baths, not as a luxury but as an absolute necessity") as reported in the *Hackney and Kingsland Gazette* of June 27, 1904. The baths were opened by the Mayor (Mr. H. B. Bird, JP) "in the presence of a large gathering of Councillors, officials and leading ratepayers, besides many ladies and gentlemen from neighbouring boroughs." Proceedings started with the chairman of the Borough Council's Baths and Wash-houses Committee, who gave a speech that contained what the newspaper describes as "many interesting details" of the progress of the scheme. The Mayor then declared the building open and expressed the hope ("as he was sure they all did") that the undertaking would "meet with the success and appreciation it deserved."

> Alderman E. J. Wakeling (Vice-chairman of the Committee) thereupon took the first plunge into the swimming bath amid loud applause, the worthy Alderman surprising everyone by swimming under water the full length of the bath.

Bravo, Alderman Wakeling! "Worthy" indeed! I picture him in a suitably modest Edwardian bathing costume yet still cutting an ever-so-slightly irreverent figure in the middle of this (from our modern perspective at least) somewhat pompous manifestation of civic pride. His plunge into the pool conveys an important lesson. There comes a time when it is good to abandon dignity. What makes me smile is not that his undignified performance exposed the dignity of the occasion as phony or bogus, but that, through a modest and appropriate kind of playfulness, it enhanced it.

Which brings us to a very important point in the argument. The assumption has been that promoting dignity is always a good thing—the issues have been whether dignity amounts to anything more than an empty piety and, if so, what respecting it might involve. But is that correct? Perhaps there are at least some times when it is proper to abandon dignity or even to attack it. We have a literary genre in which the loss of dignity—whether deliberate or unintended—is explored in its many different forms and meanings: it is called "comedy." George Orwell, no less, saw that in comedy the connection between humor and the loss of dignity is central:

> If you had to define humour in a single phrase, you might define it as dignity sitting on a tintack. Whatever destroys dignity, and brings down the mighty from their seats, preferably with a bump, is funny.

Anyone who grew up in Britain during the Second World War or in the years after it will appreciate how socially significant humor can be. As Britain struggled, fitfully and by no means fully successfully, to move away from a culture of deference and hierarchy, the appearance of great works of comedy (*ITMA, Lucky Jim, The Goon Show, Beyond the Fringe, Oh What a Lovely War!, That Was the Week That Was, Monty Python's Flying Circus,* to name a few) represented moments of liberation.

The use of irreverence to strip off the patina that dignity adds to power is often painful and shocking. So important is this kind of attack on dignity, however, that we ought, in my opinion, to resist any attempt by the state to extend the duty of being dignified beyond the realm of private tact and good taste. It seems plausible enough to say that the "dignity of the human person" should be protected by the power of the state if we understand by the dignity of the human person their inner transcendental kernel—whatever it is about us that founds our claim to be of intrinsic value. But the case is far more dubious when that means giving the state the power to enforce the duty of being respectful to oneself and others—perhaps even of being respectful toward that abstract entity, the state itself. (Article 161 of the Ukraine penal code, for example, provides for imprisonment for up to two years for the "humiliation of national honour and dignity.") We are coming close—frighteningly close—to those laws against *lèse-majesté* that tyrants have traditionally used to defend themselves.

Yet if people in democratic societies must be free to show irreverence, how does that square with the duty to treat others *with dignity*? Our duty to respect the humanity in someone's person remains (in some ways, it is even more important) when dealing with people toward whom we have every right to feel disrespect—criminals, most obviously. Like the Christian injunction to hate the sin but love the sinner, it is a very hard distinction to live by, however. Clearly, certain kinds of humiliating punishment are always unacceptable, yet how can we punish people without humiliating them? How can being deprived of one's liberty and subjected to constant surveillance fail to be humiliating? What is more, the humiliating message expressed by punishment is not an unwanted side effect. It is part of the punishment itself. The state is not just saying to the criminal: you've contracted a debt to society, now is the time to pay up. In convicting and punishing a criminal the state is publicly holding his or her action up for condemnation.

Two points should not be forgotten, however. First, there is an important discrepancy between the situation of those who hold power and those who don't. Traditionally, of course, these things worked top-down. People would be punished for not showing what was thought to be the proper respect for the dignified status of a king, an aristocrat, or a judge—to their social superiors in general. But in a democratic society things ought to be just the other way round: it is the powerful who should be required to express respect for the ordinary citizen, not citizens for the powerful. It is one thing for me to mock the head of state; quite another for the head of state to mock me. This is why the preservation of dignity in the sense of treating others with dignity is especially important when the state is exercising its most extreme power against them—punishing criminals or using violence to fight in war. Secondly, the fact that something is wrong doesn't always mean that it is right for the state to prohibit it. Admittedly, many attacks on dignity are tasteless, shocking, and distressing, not liberatingly subversive. Yet we may have to accept them for the sake of those that are.

This need to balance competing claims becomes lost from sight as soon as dignity is represented as an inner transcendental kernel, a core of value that must be protected above all else. To illustrate, let me anticipate some of the discussion later in this chapter by taking an example involving the German Verfassungsgericht (Supreme

Court). In 1987 the Verfassungsgericht upheld a conviction against a satirical magazine that had depicted the prominent politician Franz-Josef Strauss (the long-standing leader of the Christlich-Soziale Union) as a copulating pig. In the judgment of the court, "The depiction of sexual behaviour which forms part of the defensible kernel of his intimate life aims to devalue the individual in question as a person and deprive him of his dignity as a human being" (BVerfGE, 75, 36). But political caricatures are *supposed* to challenge the dignity of those they depict, and so, no doubt, they "devalue the individual in question." Is this not simply the kind of rude and tasteless thing that powerful people (and Strauss was certainly that at the time) ought to put up with in a democracy?

The right to behave disrespectfully is certainly a right to be used with tact and care. Perhaps there are even limits to what can be allowed (it makes sense to think that such limits might be drawn more narrowly in Germany, with its shameful history of hateful speech leading to persecution, than in other democratic societies). But what should be rejected is the idea that insulting and distressing speech automatically violates the essential kernel of what is valuable about human beings, so that to permit it would be to "deprive [Herr Strauss] of his dignity as a human being." This is, I think, the serious lesson to be taken from the case of M. Wackenheim. My suspicion is that, having left open the content of the idea of human dignity as a fundamental foundation for morality, those whose business it was to apply the concept of dignity in a legal context ended up giving it content by drawing on the very different concept of the dignified—requiring M. Wackenheim to behave in a dignified way. Yet, at the same time, this requirement was represented as a matter of the inviolable core of the individual. And this is a huge mistake, not only because it risks denying the citizen the right to behave disrespectfully toward things that she believes do not deserve respect, but because the quality of being dignified does not extend universally. Surely no one who subscribes to the idea that human dignity is a fundamental value and requires the protection of the state would deny that a young child falls within the scope of that protection. But what is less dignified than a two-year-old? One could, I suppose, argue that the child has grace. But dignity? Definitely not!

II. Germany

"Dignity" appears in laws and judicial decisions in many different legal systems as well as in international covenants and declarations on human rights, but no country has gone as far as Germany in integrating dignity into its legal system. As stated in the Grundgesetz (Basic Law) of the Federal Republic, the inviolable dignity of human beings is a fundamental constitutional principle. The Weimar constitution already made reference to dignity, but by elevating dignity into the first item in the first article of its Grundgesetz, the Federal Republic ensured that it would be central to German law. The first two clauses of Article 1 read in the official translation:

(1) Human dignity is inviolable [*unantast-bar*]. To respect it and protect it is the duty of all state power.

(2) The German people therefore acknowledge inviolable [*unverletzlichen*] and inalienable human rights as the basis of every community, of peace and of justice in the world.

(Note here that there are two different German words, both translated as "inviolable." Some people suggest that there is an important difference in meaning between the two.)

Article 1 of the Grundgesetz has been invoked by the Bundesverfassungsgericht (Constitutional Court) in many different contexts: for instance, to reject the idea of life sentences with no possibility of release (the death penalty itself was never part of the law in the Federal Republic), to place limits on state surveillance of private residences, to block the proposed compulsory gathering of census data, to uphold bans on peep shows, as well as, recently, to strike down a law permitting the shooting down of hijacked airliners to prevent their being used by terrorists in suicidal attacks. The courts have also agreed on a list of actions that violate human dignity—torture, slavery, genocide, subjection to humiliating or inhuman punishment, kidnap, stigmatization, the destruction of so-called "valueless life," and human experimentation, for example. The interpretation of dignity by the German courts has, naturally, been very complex, but the principles behind it are, I think, revealing.

Before looking for them, we should remember first the circumstances under which the Grundgesetz came into being. Its planning and framing in 1948 and 1949 coincided with the beginning of the Cold War. In response to increasing conflict with the Soviet Union (the blockade of Berlin that led to the Berlin Airlift ended in May 1949, the same month that the Grundgesetz came into force), the Western occupying powers and the Benelux countries insisted that the western German states should come together as a single state. The West Germans themselves, however, were reluctant to do so, not wanting to appear to accept the *de facto* division of Germany into two as having any legitimacy. Hence the choice of the name "Basic Law" rather than "Constitution" was intended to reflect what the West Germans hoped would be the new state's provisional status. There were two important requirements for the Grundgesetz. First, it must set a clear line between the new German state and its predecessors—most obviously, to separate itself from the atrocities of the Nazi state. But it was important too for the Bundesrepublik to establish a political identity that would differentiate it from its rival to the east (the German Democratic Republic was brought into being in October 1949). The idea that state power should be directed to "respecting and defending" the human dignity and that "therefore" human rights were to be recognized as "inviolable and inalienable" can be seen as responding to both of these issues.

The Grundgesetz was agreed upon by political representatives from the individual German states (the Western Allies stood somewhat in the background, requiring that the text be submitted for their approval but not being directly involved in debate). Those representatives were for the most part composed of members of the two parties that would dominate German politics in the post-war era, the Christian Democrats (CDU) and the Social Democrats (SPD). The Catholic influence through politicians such as Konrad Adenauer (who was to be the first federal chancellor) was very strong, but the adoption of Article 1 of the Grundgesetz was a clear example of "overlapping consensus" in operation: the adoption of a text framed in terms designed to be acceptable to both religious and secular participants in debate. All these elements have played a role in governing how dignity has been interpreted.

III. The Kantian Background: The Formula of Humanity

The Grundgesetz's principle that dignity is an inviolable feature of personhood can indeed be traced back to Kant. Kant writes in the *Metaphysics of Morals*:

> Humanity itself is a dignity; for a man cannot be used merely as a means by any man (either by others or even by himself) but must always be used at the same time as an end. It is just in this that his dignity (personhood [*Persönlichkeit*]) consists, by which he raises himself above all other beings in the world that are not men and yet can be used, and so over all *things*. (*Ak.* 6:462)

And humanity in our persons (as embodiments of the moral law) is explicitly described as "inviolable" in the *Critique of Practical Reason:*

> The moral law is *holy* (inviolable [*unverletzlich*]).
> A human being is indeed unholy enough but
> the *humanity* in his person must be holy to him.
> (*Ak.* 5:87)

Moreover, as we saw in Chapter 1, personhood, for Kant, is morally foundational—it is "the ground of determinate laws" (*Ak.* 4:428). The Kantian roots of the Grundgesetz have been emphasized by commentators from the outset. The Catholic legal scholar Günter Dürig, for example, echoes a famous phrase of Kant's in a much-quoted sentence of his 1958 commentary:

> Human dignity is violated when the individual
> human being [*der konkrete Mensch*] is reduced to
> a mere means, to a replaceable magnitude [*ver-
> tretbare Größe*].

Dürig's so-called object formula *(Objektformel)* has been the starting point for the discussion of dignity in German law, so it makes sense to ask how we should understand the Kantian thought it expresses. Would a proper interpretation of Kant enable us to draw the boundaries of "dignity" in a clear and principled way and give us "determinate laws"?

In one very famous formulation of the "categorical imperative" (the Formula of Humanity, as it is conventionally called) Kant writes: "So act that you treat humanity, whether in your own person or in the person of any other, always at the same time as an end, never merely as a means" (*Ak.* 4:429). What exactly the Formula of Humanity amounts to has been discussed endlessly in the academic literature, of course. In offering my own very brief account of it, I shall bypass some of these details to bring out as clearly as I can what I take to be its deep problems. With this in mind, I make no apology for starting with something obvious. The Formula of Humanity contains two elements: first, it says that you must treat humanity "always . . . as an end" and, second, "never merely as a means." Let me take that second element first and ask: what is it to treat a person "merely as a means"?

One way of dealing with people that indisputably treats them merely as a means is treating them purely as physical objects. Suppose that it is a cold and windy day and a group of people are standing together in a line, waiting for a bus. You go and stand behind them so that they act as a windbreak for you. Clearly, you are using them as a means and nothing else—they are advancing your interests and you are not acknowledging them as persons (indeed, your interests would be just as well served if they were inanimate pieces of wood). Nevertheless, although your using the bus queue as a windbreak is to use the people in it as a means only, it does not seem that you are doing anything morally objectionable. After all, although you are taking advantage of them, you haven't disadvantaged them in any way. They would still be standing there, just as cold and miserable (but no more so) if you weren't there at all.

Such cases of treating other people as mere things are very rare, however—mostly just the product of philosophers' capacity to come up with ingenious examples. Real-life cases are more complex. Remember that Kant doesn't say that we can't treat people as means (more strictly, treat the humanity in their persons as means) at all. Indeed, it would be hard to imagine how social life could be carried on if we weren't allowed to treat one another as means at least some of the time (the bus driver is a means to getting you to work, the IT support person is a means to getting the network running, and so on). Kant's prohibition is against treating them as *means only*. Usually when we use other people, we treat them in ways that are only possible because they are more than things—it is their human capacities that make them useful. And this is still true when we use people in ways that are morally unacceptable: you can't bully, deceive, or exploit a piece of wood. But that brings a new interpretive difficulty. When I am using a person in such a way—lying to them, for example—aren't I also at the same time in some sense *recognizing* them and, for that reason, treating them as a person? I am, after all, talking to them and expecting them to understand me. So here is the next stage of the problem: if making use of a person normally requires us to recognize them *as* a person in some minimal way at least (to treat them as a person rather than an inanimate object), how much further do we have to go until we are no longer treating them as "mere means"?

One obvious idea is that people are being treated as mere means, despite being recognized as persons, if we

behave toward them in ways that give no independent weight to their interests (their desires or their well-being). In this way, a slave-holder might be said to treat her slaves as "means only" if she does nothing to advance their welfare that isn't also a way of advancing her own interests. So perhaps we can infer from that that we are not treating people as mere means provided that we do give some independent weight to their interests. But that idea will not work. What if the slave-owner uses her slaves harshly but nevertheless does not exploit them to the last degree? Would that not satisfy Kant's criterion? Yet evidently that does not make slave-owning morally acceptable. The philosopher Derek Parfit tells a story about his own mother who was robbed by river pirates in China. The pirates allowed her to keep her wedding ring. Clearly, this little element of chivalry shows that the pirates were not treating Mrs. Parfit as a means only in the sense of taking everything that she had. Equally clearly, however, it did not make it all right for them to rob her.

To sum up so far: we have seen that there could be a case in which it seems to be actually morally acceptable to use people as means only in the sense of treating them as mere things (using them as a windbreak). On the other hand, neither the mere fact of acknowledging people's agency in interacting with them nor that of giving some weight to their interests (both of which seem to be reasonable ways of making sense of the idea that people are not being treated as "means *only*") are sufficient to make actions morally acceptable. There are many other, more complex, suggestions in the literature, of course, but I think

that we have done enough for now to establish that the difficulties in applying the idea of not treating people as means only run deep. What about the positive idea that we should treat them "as ends"?

In the paragraphs preceding his statement of the Formula of Humanity, Kant introduces the idea that human beings are "ends in themselves" in terms of a contrast between those things that have value conditionally, based on our inclinations, and those that have value unconditionally:

> Suppose there was something the *existence of which in itself* has an absolute worth, something which *as an end in itself* could be the ground of determinate laws; then in it, and in it alone, would be the ground of a possible categorical imperative, that is, of a practical law.
>
> Now I say that the human being and in general every rational being exists as an end in itself, not merely as a means to be used by this or that will at its direction; instead, he must in all his actions, whether directed to himself or also to other rational beings, always be regarded *at the same time as an end.* (Ak. 4:428)

Even non-rational living beings that exist independently of our will, Kant says, still "have only a relative worth, as means, and are therefore called *things* [*Sachen*]" (Ak. 4:428). Rational beings, on the other hand, "are called *persons* because their nature already marks them out as an end in itself, that is, as something that may not be used merely as a means, and hence to that extent limits all choice [*sofern alle Willkür einschränkt*] (and is an object of respect)" (*Ak.* 4:428). Persons, the embodiments of morality, have absolute value independent of what the facts about human desires or choices happen to be. The absolute value that human beings embody—namely, the moral law—is an object of respect and, at the same time (or so Kant says) functions as the "ground of determinate laws."

If human beings really are ends of this kind, how should we treat them, however? A good way to see the difficulty is by contrasting Kant's view with that of utilitarianism, the doctrine that happiness is the sole ultimate good. The utilitarian too makes a distinction between those ends that have value relative to the desires or choices of individuals (their personal happiness) and what has value independently—general happiness. So, for utilitarianism, general happiness is an end in itself. Yet happiness is an end that we know how to promote: the more the better! By contrast, although you might say that human beings' moral personhood is an "end," it isn't at all clear how we should go about furthering it. Personhood is not a state of affairs to be brought about—something we can get closer to or move away from. Human beings already have the dignity of personhood inalienably, so long as they are moral agents. How to treat human beings *as ends* thus appears to be another open question. From which I conclude that neither of the two parts of the Formula of Humanity gives us an obvious or easy way of settling what is and what isn't morally permissible.

Of course, Kant himself did not believe that his moral theory lacked content. The Formula of Humanity is introduced in the *Groundwork* after Kant has presented his categorical imperative in another, equally celebrated, formulation, the Formula of Universal Law: "act only in accordance with that maxim through which you can at the same time will that it become a universal law" (*Ak.* 4:421). Whereas the Formula of Humanity concentrates on identifying something that has intrinsic value (human beings as embodiments of the moral law), the Formula of Universal Law explores the structure of rational willing. Those acts that are prohibited, according to Kant, are prohibited either because we cannot even *think* of their maxims (the principle behind them) being a universal law of nature or because we cannot *will* that their maxims become laws ("because such a will would contradict itself"; *Ak.* 4:424). Kant then follows both the statement of the Formula of Universal Law and the Formula of Humanity with four cases of moral duty that, he claims, can be derived equally well from the categorical imperative on either of the two formulations. These four cases are supposed to be examples of duties of four fundamental kinds, divided on two axes: duties to ourselves and duties to others; perfect duties and imperfect duties. Thus the prohibition of suicide is a perfect duty to ourselves, the duty of promise-keeping a perfect duty to others, the duty of developing our capacities an imperfect duty to ourselves, and the duty of helping those in need an imperfect duty to others.

Reasonably enough, then, Kant's modern interpreters have used the Formula of Universal Law, with its emphasis on willing, to help specify the Formula of Humanity. The contemporary Kant scholar Christine Korsgaard's explanation is that we can understand how humanity comes to be "an end in itself" by considering how things in general become ends:

> What was in question was the source of good- ness of an end—the goodness say, of some or- dinary object of inclination. This source was traced to the power of rationally choosing ends, exercised in this case on this end. So when Kant says rational nature or humanity is an end in itself, it is the power of rational choice that he is referring to, and in particular, the power to set an end (to make something an end by confer- ring the status of goodness on it) and pursue it by rational means.

It is our capacity to confer value on things by choosing and willing that makes us agents, and the fact that we can do that rationally makes us moral agents, ends in ourselves, according to Korsgaard. Onora O'Neill makes a similar kind of connection between the value of human beings as ends in themselves and their capacity for ratio- nal agency:

> Things cannot act, so can have no maxims, so cannot consent or dissent from the ways in which they are used. . . . When we impose our wills on things we do not prevent, restrict or damage their agency—for they have none. . . . By contrast, if we treat other agents as mere means, we do prevent, damage or restrict their agency.

> We use them as props or implements in our own
> projects, in ways that preempt their willing
> and deny them the *possibility* of collaboration
> or consent—or dissent. It is not merely that we
> may act in ways to which they *do not* consent; we
> act on maxims to which they *could not* consent.

Korsgaard and O'Neill (both students of John Rawls)
are two of the most sophisticated modern advocates of
Kantian moral theory. Their accounts of what it is to
treat human beings as ends in themselves connect to
human beings' nature as rational agents—in Korsgaard's
case to the power of rational choice to confer value on
things, in O'Neill's to the requirement to treat individuals
in ways to which they could (rationally) consent (accounts
that, of course, can easily be understood as complemen-
tary to one another). Both give what we can call, broadly
speaking, *voluntaristic* accounts of what it is for human beings to be ends in themselves—not, of course, in the sense
that what has absolute value is this or that act of arbitrary
choice, but that human beings are intrinsically valuable
because they have *both* the capacity to will in general *and* to
constrain their willing by principles of reason.

One explanation, then, for why the interpretation of
dignity in German constitutional law has not just been a
matter of giving the Formula of Humanity concrete legal
articulation is simply how difficult it is to fix what the
Formula amounts to in order to derive "determinate
laws" from it. But that is only part of the story. We should
not forget the different roles played by dignity in the

Grundgesetz and the Formula of Humanity in Kantian ethics. The Formula of Humanity is one formulation of the Kantian categorical imperative. That is, it embodies (or, at least, forms part of) a comprehensive moral principle that, properly interpreted (or so Kant would have us believe), reveals all the different kinds of moral duty that apply to individuals: duties to ourselves, duties to others, perfect duties, and imperfect duties. Dignity when it is incorporated in a constitutional law like the German Grundgesetz necessarily plays a quite different, much more limited role. As part of the legal framework of a liberal-democratic state, it acts, as laws do, to establish norms for state action and constrain the private action of individuals. "Dignity" in a constitutional law simply sets boundaries for individuals' behavior beyond which the state is called on to exercise its coercive powers and intervene. Unlike the Categorical Imperative, which lays out principles prescribing how individuals should act in general, "dignity" in a constitutional law simply establishes boundaries for their behavior beyond which the state is called upon to intervene.

IV. Catholicism and the Grundgesetz

But another reason—and a more important one, to my mind—why we cannot understand the interpretation of dignity in the Grundgesetz as just the attempt to turn the Kantian distinction between treating people as ends and as means only into legal practice is the significance for German law of another, non-Kantian tradition of ethical thought, specifically that of Catholicism. The Bundesrepublik, of course, understands itself as a modern democratic state in which religious belief plays no political role. Nevertheless, the influence of religion (and of Catholicism in particular) on law and politics has always been great. The main German political parties of the center-right—the Christlich Demokratische Union (CDU) and its Bavarian ally, the Christlich-Soziale Union (CSU)—have an explicitly Christian orientation. According to a survey carried out in 2005, 51 percent of the membership of the CDU are Catholic, 33.3 percent are Protestant, and 15.7 percent are not members of a church. The CSU, as a regional Bavarian party, will undoubtedly be even more heavily Catholic. The religious influence was particularly strong immediately after the war, for understandable historical reasons. Most of the (relatively few) public figures on the political right who had not been wholly discredited by their actions under National Socialism had strong religious affiliations (most obviously, as already mentioned, Konrad Adenauer). Moreover, there has traditionally been a very strong Catholic presence in the German legal profession (both as members of the judiciary and as academic lawyers). Günter Dürig apart, Ernst-Wolfgang Böckenförde, arguably the most influential member of the Constitutional Court (he sat as a judge from 1983–1996), is a Catholic (as well as being a pupil of Carl Schmitt and a member of the SPD).

As we saw in the previous chapter, "dignity" played a major role in Catholic ethical and social thought in the nineteenth century as an alternative to the idea of human rights. It was used (by Leo XIII, for example) to oppose various democratic and egalitarian ideas in favor of a conception of society and family as embodying an (allegedly) divinely ordained descending hierarchy of authority. In the late nineteenth and early twentieth centuries the Church identified socialism as the pernicious further consequence of adherence to democratic ideas of popular sovereignty. The Catholic Church's opposition to democratic egalitarianism made it less critical toward various radical right-wing—fascist and falangist—movements, and this (to say the least) compromised its effectiveness in opposing National Socialism. To put it bluntly, the nineteenth-century Catholic notion of dignity was part of the Catholic Church's long war against the principles of the French Revolution.

By the time of the Grundgesetz (and the Universal Declaration of Human Rights) that fight was finally over and Catholic social teaching had undergone a very significant (if largely silent) re-orientation. At the beginning of the Cold War the Church was, understandably, focusing principally on its opposition to Communism. Catholics were now prepared to associate human dignity with equal rights and democracy and so to ally themselves with secular liberalism against the regimes to the East. Thus the Church was happy to endorse Article 1 of the Grundgesetz with its emphasis on the pre-eminent place of human dignity and the inference that dignity ("therefore") functions as the ground for the assertion of "inviolable" and "inalienable" human rights held equally by all. This fundamental transformation of Catholic social teaching would be entrenched, finally, by the Second Vatican Council. (Interestingly, at the time of the founding of the Bundesrepublik not everyone seems to have got the memo. The Bavarian State Parliament, dominated by the CSU, declined to ratify the Grundgesetz—although they voted that it should be accepted if more than two-thirds of the West German states voted in its favor, as was indeed the case. One of the parliamentary voices raised in opposition came from a Catholic priest who objected, just as Leo XIII himself would have done, to the statement in Article 20 that "all state power derives from the people.")

But although the conception of dignity promulgated by Catholics after the Second World War was essentially egalitarian and favorable to the idea of human rights, it by no means represented the endorsement of a Kantian conception of morality. Nowhere is this clearer than in the answer given to the basic question: who are the bearers of human dignity? Kant, as we have seen, agrees that "humanity itself is a dignity" (*Ak*. 6:642). But, for Kant, the inviolability of "humanity in [one's] person" consists precisely in our moral agency, the presence in us of the "holy" moral law (*Ak*. 5:87). To take this view and to tie our being ends in ourselves to, as Korsgaard puts it, "the power to set an end (to make something an end by conferring the status of goodness on it) and pursue it by rational means" seems to draw the boundaries of personhood quite narrowly: it restricts it to those human beings who are actively capable of exercising rational agency. This is something that has been vehemently opposed by Catholics. As is well known, the Catholic Church asserts that the dignity of the human person exists fully "from the moment of conception." In maintaining that position the Church has argued that setting the boundaries more narrowly is a product of the pernicious modern tendency to locate the origin of value in human willing.

In two extremely important encyclicals from the 1990s, *Veritatis Splendor* (1993) and *Evangelium Vitae* (1995), John Paul II argued against the voluntarism that he identified as pervasive in contemporary, secular moral thought. (At this time, the German, Joseph Ratzinger—later, as Benedict XVI, John Paul II's successor—was Prefect of the Sacred Congregation for the Doctrine of the Faith, the Pope's senior lieutenant in matters of faith and doctrine, and there is every reason to think that he had a major influence on the two encyclicals.) *Veritatis Splendor* is a long and complex document that contains a general account of the Catholic view of morality. Its positive doctrines are clear enough and will come as little surprise—that morality is divine in origin and immutable, that morality is embodied in a natural law that is accessible to human reason in the form of the conscience and, in more perfect form, through the Church and the revelation of scripture. More interesting, however, is John Paul II's diagnosis of the contemporary moral situation—the competing alternatives against which Catholic moral teaching must contend.

Veritatis Splendor's engagement with contemporary currents of moral thought centers on the Catholic understanding of human freedom. As John Paul II writes, "The human issues most frequently debated and differently re-

solved in contemporary moral reflection are all closely related, albeit in various ways, to a crucial issue: *human freedom*" (31). The Pope starts by accepting that the affirmation
of human freedom is a fundamental feature of modern
society. "People today have a particularly strong sense of
freedom" (31), he writes (uncontroversially enough). Indeed, this is something that he endorses: "This heightened
sense of the dignity of the human person and of his or
her uniqueness, and of the respect due to the journey of
conscience, certainly represents one of the positive achievements of modern culture" (32). But (there's always a "but"
in such cases, isn't there?) the modern emphasis on freedom carries dangers with it, the Pope warns. "This perception, authentic as it is, has been expressed in a number of
more or less adequate ways, some of which, however, di-
verge from the truth about man as a creature and the image of God, and thus need to be corrected and purified in
the light of faith. Certain currents of modern thought have
gone so far as to *exalt freedom to such an extent that it becomes
an absolute, which would then be the source of values.* This is the
direction taken by doctrines which have lost the sense of
the transcendent or which are explicitly atheist" (31, 32).
Seeing human freedom as an "absolute" and at the same
time as "the source of values" is to sever morality from
truth and to set off down the path that leads toward
relativism. Although expressed in somewhat opaque
"Popespeak," it seems fairly evident that the Pope is making Kantianism the target of his criticism here.

Two years later, John Paul II followed up these general
considerations regarding the nature of morality with a

sharply worded reassertion of the Church's teaching on matters of sexuality and bio-ethics. At its center is an argument in which he identifies what he claims to be a fundamental contradiction between the democratic affirmation of human rights and the "culture of death" prevalent in modern Western societies in which abortion has been legalized:

> The process which once led to discovering the idea of "human rights"—rights inherent in every person and prior to any Constitution and State legislation—is today marked by a surprising contradiction. Precisely in an age when the inviolable rights of the person are solemnly proclaimed and the value of life is publicly affirmed, the very right to life is being denied or trampled upon, especially at the more significant moments of existence: the moment of birth and the moment of death. On the one hand, the various declarations of human rights and the many initiatives inspired by these declarations show that at the global level there is a growing moral sensitivity, more alert to acknowledging the value and dignity of every individual as a human being, without any distinction of race, nationality, religion, political opinion or social class. On the other hand, these noble proclamations are unfortunately contradicted by a tragic repudiation of them in practice. This denial is still more distressing, indeed more scandalous, precisely because it is

> occurring in a society which makes the affir-
> mation and protection of human rights its
> primary objective and its boast. How can these
> repeated affirmations of principle be recon-
> ciled with the continual increase and wide-
> spread justification of attacks on human life?
> How can we reconcile these declarations with
> the refusal to accept those who are weak and
> needy, or elderly, or those who have just been
> conceived? These attacks go directly against re-
> spect for life and they represent a direct threat
> to the entire culture of human rights. (18)

It is striking to see the Catholic Church in the late twentieth century presenting its ethical views in the language
of universal human rights—something that would have
been quite unthinkable a century previously. The Church's
objection now is not to the denial of social hierarchy and
divine authority implicit in the "culture of human rights"
but that human rights are not being consistently applied,
that they exclude "those who have just been conceived."

In the next section of the encyclical, John Paul II sets
himself the task of exploring the "roots of this remarkable contradiction." In the light of *Veritatis Splendor* it will
be no surprise to learn that he sees it as springing from a
voluntaristic and subjectivistic conception of the nature
of value:

> We can find [the roots of this contradiction] in
> an overall assessment of a cultural and moral
> nature, beginning with the mentality which
> carries the concept of subjectivity to an extreme

and even distorts it, and recognizes as a subject of rights only the person who enjoys full or at least incipient autonomy and who emerges from a state of total dependence on others. But how can we reconcile this approach with the exaltation of man as a being who is "not to be used"? The theory of human rights is based precisely on the affirmation that the human person, unlike animals and things, cannot be subjected to domination by others. We must also mention the mentality which tends to equate personal dignity with the capacity for verbal and explicit, or at least perceptible, communication. It is clear that on the basis of these presuppositions there is no place in the world for anyone who, like the unborn or the dying, is a weak element in the social structure, or for anyone who appears completely at the mercy of others and radically dependent on them, and can only communicate through the silent language of a profound sharing of affection. In this case it is force which becomes the criterion for choice and action in interpersonal relations and in social life. But this is the exact opposite of what a State ruled by law, as a community in which the "reasons of force" are replaced by the "force of reason," historically intended to affirm. (19)

All in all then, the Catholic Church agrees with the central place given to human freedom in the modern world and the idea that human beings, as embodiments of "dignity," are also the bearers of universal and inalienable rights, but it denies the view (which it associates with the modern understanding of freedom) that autonomy is essential to the possession of rights or that moral values should be seen as being in some way the product of human beings' power of choosing or willing. Clearly, there is still a fundamental disagreement between modern Catholicism and Kantianism. On the "voluntaristic" account of Kant (as I termed it) presented by interpreters such as Korsgaard and O'Neill, the ultimate source of value is human beings' capacity to set and agree to ends rationally, and the pre-eminent bearers of value are human beings themselves insofar as they embody and exercise that capacity. Plainly, John Paul II completely rejects both of these ideas.

At the same time, significantly, in both of these encyclicals John Paul II himself uses language that is strongly reminiscent of Kant. Thus in the passage just quoted from *Evangelium Vitae* he talks about man as a "being 'who is not to be used'" or "subjected to the domination of others." In *Veritatis Splendor* there is a passage that even more clearly echoes Kant:

> It is in the light of the dignity of the person—
> a dignity which must be affirmed for its own
> sake—that reason grasps the specific moral value
> of certain goods towards which the person is
> naturally inclined. And since the person cannot
> be reduced to a freedom which is self-designing,

but entails a particular spiritual and bodily
structure, the primordial moral requirement of
loving and *respecting the person as an end and never
as a mere means* also implies, by its very nature,
respect for certain fundamental goods, without
which one would fall into relativism and arbi-
trariness. (48, my emphasis)

This passage (somewhat coded again) is interesting if
we read it in the light of the "voluntarist" interpretation of
Kant. On that view, the dignity of human beings is indeed
to be identified with their possession of a "self-designing"
freedom—the power to set ends and to pursue them by rational means. Such freedom, however, is not arbitrary but
constrained by the fact that the freedom of each must co-
exist with the freedom of all others. The Pope, on the other
hand, is affirming the existence of constraints on human
volition other than those set by the volitions of other individuals. A "particular spiritual and *bodily* structure" sets
certain fundamental goods as ends which must rationally
be acknowledged. In this way the Catholic Church can be
read as offering its own interpretation of the Formula of
Humanity: treat human beings in ways that are conso-
nant with their place within a divinely established natural
order.

V. Interpreting the Grundgesetz

It has often been pointed out (by the founders of the Federal Republic themselves, not least) that it is possible for

people of different views to accept common legal, moral, or political conceptions without also agreeing on their philosophical foundations. Though this is true enough, things become more problematic when it comes to applying such conceptions in practice. Interpreters need some idea of what the point of a conception is in order to apply it, and where else to look for that than in the principles behind it?

In the case of dignity, the problem looks to be especially acute. Yes, you might say, Kantians and Catholics agree that human beings have "dignity"—that is, that some kind of "absolute," even "inviolable," inner core of value inheres in them—but where do we go from there? If dignity is the value that something has in itself, as Aquinas and Kant in their different ways both assert, how must we behave toward a being that embodies that value? What rights follow from it? And what does it mean to deprive someone of dignity? If dignity were an alienable possession of mine, then we could describe how I could be deprived of it, but if my dignity is essential to me as a human being, then, presumably, it will remain with me whatever others might do. When we talk of people being "deprived" of their inalienable rights, what we mean, clearly, is not that those rights somehow disappear but that people are being denied the opportunity to exercise them. What might it mean to "exercise" (or be prevented from exercising) our inalienable dignity?

And yet, for all of these potential difficulties, there has been much less open conflict over the interpretation of dignity in the German courts than one might have expected. The reasons for this strike me as significant.

On some central issues where Kantianism and Catholic ethical thought are in conflict, the Bundesverfassungsgericht has clearly interpreted dignity along Catholic (or, at least, religion-friendly) lines. This is most apparent when it comes to the boundaries of dignity—who are its bearers? In 1975 the Verfassungsgericht vetoed a legislative proposal to legalize abortion (under certain circumstances) as a violation of Article 1, paragraph 1 (the dignity clause), and Article 2, paragraph 2 (the right to life), of the Grundgesetz. Its judgment affirmed the fetus's right to protection on the ground of human dignity in unambiguous language:

> The life that is developing in the maternal body stands under the protection of the constitution (Grundgesetz, Art. 2, Para. 2, Clause 1; Art. 1., Para. 1) as an independent legal entity [*Rechtsgut*]. The protective duty of the state not only prohibits the state from direct interference with the developing life but enjoins the state to protect and promote it. The obligation of the state to protect the developing life exists also in relation to its mother. (BVerfGE, 39, 1)

The court revisited the issue of abortion in 1993 when the question of finding a common legal framework with the former East German states arose (the German Democratic Republic had had a more permissive abortion law). In its judgment, the court once again affirmed its previous position in equally forceful language:

> Human dignity is already an attribute of unborn human life, not just human life after birth

or with a developed personality.... [During] pregnancy the unborn is something individual, something established in its genetic identity and hence its uniqueness and irreplaceability. It is indivisible life that, in the process of growth and articulation, does not develop *into* a human being [*Mensch*] but develops *as* a human being. However the different phases of antenatal life may be interpreted from a biological, philosophical or theological standpoint, it is a question of the indispensable stages in the development of an individual human being. Where human life exists [*menschliches Leben*] human dignity belongs to it. (BVerfGE, 88, 203)

The court's rigoristic stance regarding the extension of human dignity to fetuses at all stages of development is strongly out of line with German public opinion. A 2005 poll showed 64 percent of the German public agreeing with the statement "If a woman does not want children, she should be able to have an abortion" (for comparison, 66 percent agreed in the UK and 62 percent in an average of ten European countries). The outcome has been a remarkable compromise (all the more remarkable in that it appears to have been accepted by the German public with almost no objection). The court, while re-affirming that abortion is illegal *(rechtswidrig),* has nevertheless accepted that abortion should not be punishable *(strafbar)* provided that it takes place in defined circumstances (generally, within the first twelve weeks and after the pregnant woman has participated in an independent counseling session). In other words, the court permits the state not to protect the right to life that (allegedly) flows from the fetus's inviolable human dignity, but at the same time reserves for itself the authority to set legal limits beyond which what looks like the state's abdication of its primary constitutional duty may not go. Schopenhauer would, no doubt, be smiling!

VI. Daschner and the Air Safety Law

"Deontological" is a label applied by philosophers to moral theories that hold that, in some circumstances at least, the right thing to do is not simply to perform that action that will produce the most good. Clearly, conceptions of dignity that see human beings as having a special kind of "inviolable" value that overrides other claims are deontological, and both Kantianism and Catholic ethics are strongly in agreement about this. Both believe in certain prohibitions that hold even if the end produced by violating them would be (an increased amount of) good. The great difficulty for deontological theories, however, is what to do when deontological claims (apparently) conflict with one another. Two cases involving the interpretation of dignity in German law illustrate how deep these problems are.

One, which came before the district court in Frankfurt (the Landgericht) in 2005, was the so-called "Daschner trial." Wolfgang Daschner, deputy chief of police in Frankfurt at the time, had been in charge of the investigation of the kidnapping and (as it turned out) murder of Jakob von

Metzler, the eleven-year-old son of a very wealthy local family. The presumed kidnapper, Magnus Gäfgen, had been arrested after being observed retrieving a ransom payment, but he refused to admit his guilt or reveal where the child was hidden. The police, who were convinced (rightly) that Gäfgen was acting alone, believed that it was a matter of extreme urgency to find Jakob, who would be without food or drink (in fact, the child was already dead). Daschner therefore threatened Gäfgen that, unless he revealed where Jakob was, he would be subjected to very severe (though not physically damaging) pain. In response to this threat, the kidnapper speedily revealed the hiding place—alas, to no avail.

In a judgment of great insight and humanity, the court condemned Daschner and fined (but did not imprison) him. The court acknowledged both the admirable motivation behind his actions and the extraordinary pressure he was under. Nevertheless, what he did, in the judgment of the court, represented not just a plain violation of the penal code, but also a breach of the dignity clause of the Grundgesetz in even threatening Gäfgen with torture. The court explicitly rejected the idea that the dignity of the suspected kidnapper could be weighed against claims made by the dignity of the kidnapped child. Nor did it accept the analogy with the police's authorization to use deadly force to save the lives of third parties who are in mortal danger *(finaler Rettungsschuss)*.

Similar issues were raised by a case that came to the Verfassungsgericht itself in 2005 and on which it gave its verdict in February 2006. The case concerned a law passed in the wake of the terrorist atrocities of September 2001, the so-called Air Safety Law (Luftsicherheitsgesetz). This law empowered the state to authorize the shooting down by the air force of a hijacked airliner if there were overwhelming reason to believe that it would be used as a weapon to cause further casualties. The Verfassungsgericht, however, rejected the law as contrary to the constitution and, in particular, as a violation of the dignity of passengers and crew. To shoot down a hijacked plane would be to treat its passengers and crew in a way that denied "their quality as subjects" and was for that reason contrary to Article I, paragraph I of the constitution:

> Due to the circumstances, which cannot be controlled by them in any way, the crew and the passengers of the plane cannot escape this state action but are helpless and defenseless in the face of it with the consequence that they are shot down in a targeted manner together with the aircraft and as result of this will be killed with near certainty. Such a treatment ignores the status of the persons affected as subjects endowed with dignity and inalienable rights. By their killing being used as a means to save others, they are treated as objects and at the same time deprived of their rights; with their lives being disposed of unilaterally by the state, the persons on board the aircraft, who, as victims, are themselves in need of protection, are denied the value which is due to a

> human being for his or her own sake. (BVerfGE,
> 115, 118)

These two judgments show clearly that, in the view of the German courts, dignity rules out certain actions, despite the existence of other urgent claims. Yet the issues the judgments raise are complicated, both morally and conceptually. Why should the kidnapper's dignity make the threat to torture him impermissible when a child's life is (reasonably believed) to be at stake? Why protect the lives of the airline passengers (who will anyway die shortly) at the cost of fulfilling the project of their murderers and the lives of those on the ground against whom the terrorists are aiming the aircraft?

VII. Is There a Consistent Interpretation?

There are, or so it seems to me, four possible ways of understanding the German courts' practice in reconciling such conflicts. All four, however, face serious difficulties.

1. Dignity is being balanced. The point of deontology is that claims made by one kind of value must always override the claims of those values that are inferior. Yet what happens when we have competing claims of the same kind? Should we not weigh them against each other? You might still say that dignity is "inviolable," since dignity is not being weighed against claims of a different kind, only against itself. This is obviously the least likely interpretation, however, since the courts have repeatedly (and vehemently) denied that dignity-claims may be weighed and balanced. Moreover, it is hard to see why, if dignity-claims actually *were* being weighed against one another, the claims of the kidnap victim should fail to outweigh those of his kidnapper, or the claims of the suicide bombers' many other potential victims should not outweigh those of the passengers and crew who are doomed anyway.

On the other hand, no police force could function if there were not circumstances under which it was permitted to use coercive violence, and Germany is no exception. But if a policeman knocks me violently to the ground, he violates my bodily autonomy and, hence, (or, at least, so it seems plausible to think) violates my dignity. But does that mean that he is not permitted to knock me down if that is the only way to keep me out of the line of fire of a gunman armed with a rifle? And wouldn't the case be essentially the same if he had to knock me to the ground to save someone else? This looks like a weighing of competing dignity-claims (physical autonomy against the need to preserve life), and we might say the same thing about the Daschner Case and the Air Safety Law. It looks, at least, as if the dignity-claim of the kidnapper not to be tortured is outweighing the dignity-claim of his victim to life and safety. Likewise the dignity-claim of the hijacked passengers could be thought to be outweighing the dignity-claim to life of the potential further victims.

If dignity is really not being balanced in these cases (and the courts consistently maintain that it is not), we need some other account.

2. While dignity itself is not being balanced, the rights that are derived from dignity are. The Grundgesetz refers to dignity as the foundation of rights (Article 1, paragraph 2, refers to the "inviolable and inalienable human rights" [*unverletzlichen und unveräußerlichen Menschenrechten*] that the German people *therefore* acknowledge). Perhaps the "inviolability" [= *Unverletzlichkeit*] of those rights is not the same as the "inviolability" [= *Unantastbarkeit*] of dignity, however, and perhaps, while the former may be balanced, the latter may not.

This is evidently the interpretation that many German lawyers find most attractive, and it seems to fit well with the understanding of dignity as an inner kernel that gives value to human beings. If dignity really is just such a transcendental kernel, then in fact the idea of the inviolability of dignity becomes true pretty much by definition: it isn't clear how dignity in that sense *could* ever be violated at all. However badly we might treat people, they would still retain their intrinsic value. All we can do is fail to treat human beings in the way that their dignity requires.

Yet it is clear that the German courts do not just see dignity as a source of rights. The Verfassungsgericht commonly identifies the violation of dignity itself as a separate harm beyond the violation of some particular right derived from it. Thus, in the abortion decisions, abortion is said to violate both the fetus's right to life and its dignity, whereas in the Air Safety Law case, the court's objection to the shooting down of a hijacked airliner was not just that it would violate the passengers' and crew's rights to life but that it would violate their dignity too. If there is a separate dignity element either alongside or as part of the rights that are founded on dignity, however, the question of balance arises again. Why should the dignity-claim of Jakob von Metzler to be saved from kidnap and murder be overridden by the dignity-claim of Gäfgen, his kidnapper, not to be tortured (or even threatened with torture)?

The idea here is that dignity-claims are being compared and weighed against one another, whatever the courts might say. But perhaps, someone might argue, while the right not to be kidnapped and murdered is a right that is *derived from* dignity (in whatever mysterious way that is supposed to happen), kidnapping and murder are not themselves violations of dignity in the way that torture is. So the refusal to threaten Gäfgen with torture is not an example of one dignity-claim being used to override another dignity-claim but rather a dignity-claim being used to override a dignity-derived right.

If you find this at all plausible, let me argue against you with a ridiculous example. Imagine that Franz-Josef Strauss has been kidnapped and is being held hostage by an enemy (he had plenty). Imagine that this kidnapper requires for the safe release of his hostage that Strauss should be humiliated in some way—say, by the publication of a cartoon depicting him as a copulating pig. Now the publication of such a cartoon was, as we have seen, a direct violation of dignity, according to the court. So, by the argument just presented, if kidnapping and hostage-taking were not in themselves violations of dignity but just the violation of a right derived from dignity, and if direct dignity-claims must always override the rights derived from dignity, then it would not be permissible to save Franz-Josef Strauss by publishing the cartoon—an absurd position, you will (I hope) agree.

So we move to a third possibility.

3. Violations of dignity that are the direct result of deliberate actions are prohibited with especial stringency. One way to understand deontological prohibitions—moral limits on the ways that the general good can be promoted—is that someone (or something) affected by an action has a value (a right or, perhaps, dignity itself) that overrides reasons that may be greater in quantity but are inferior in kind. But another way of looking at deontology is from the point of view of the agent herself. Rights, in Robert Nozick's phrase, are *side-constraints;* that is, they set limits to the ways in which agents can *act.*

So, on this view, you may (indeed, must) try to save someone's life if you can, but you may not torture in order to do it. Evidently this view involves some significant complexities in the understanding of action. To put it crudely, we have to distinguish between a course of action whose aim is to save a life (but involves torture) and one that involves protecting someone from torture (but at the cost of a life). While that may seem obvious enough in this case, the many further distinctions that may be involved (between doing and allowing, intending and foreseeing, taking something as an end and as a means, between the means to an end and unwanted side effects, to name a few) lead us quickly into issues of the greatest intricacy.

Concern with the intrinsic quality of actions apart from their outcomes is a fundamental theme in both Kantianism and Catholic ethics, and it has certainly played a significant role in the German courts. There is an important difference between the ethical and legal contexts, however. In Kantianism and Catholicism, concern with the intrinsic quality of actions is motivated by the idea that certain means, even when employed for good ends, corrupt the integrity of the individual agent—an agent who, in the end, must expect to answer for her actions to a just creator-God. In dignity jurisprudence, however, the focus is not on what individual agents may do so much as on the limits that must be placed on the actions of the state and its representatives. Clearly, this complicates things even further. If it is difficult sometimes to draw the boundaries between what is the intended goal of an individual's action and what is the means, how much more so when the agent is the state?

The emphasis on setting limits to state action is, of course, both understandable and appropriate in the light of history. The atrocities of the Nazi regime took place within a legal framework that explicitly subordinated all private interests to the collective ends of the state. It left behind an extreme sensitivity to the danger of allowing the state discretion to balance its ends against those of individual citizens, even where those ends are not the monstrous ones of Nazism. From this perspective, the overwhelming power of the state can be safely managed only if its exercise is constrained by absolute limits and prohibitions. Thus, though the state has a general duty to uphold, so far as it can, the dignity of victims like Jakob von Metzler when that is under attack by third parties, there is an absolute prohibition on even threatening to take direct action to torture his kidnapper. As the judge in that case wrote, "Beware of taking the first step!"

Important though the asymmetry between what may be done actively and deliberately by the state and what it may permit to happen is, it does not seem to cover every case. Sometimes the state (apparently) directly violates dignity in defense of the dignity and rights of third parties. The *finaler Rettungsschuss* (the use of deadly force against someone who represents an immediate threat to the lives of others) involves the police taking direct steps to end a person's life in order to save third parties. Yet this is permitted under German law. Moreover, although the Verfassungsgericht deemed the Air Safety Law unconstitutional because it violated the dignity of passengers and crew, the court also went out of its way to state in its judgment that, were an aircraft to be under terrorist control without the presence of crew or passengers, it would indeed be permissible for the air force to shoot it down.

Given this, a fourth interpretation suggests itself.

4. Dignity can be forfeited as a consequence of criminal actions. The idea that criminal behavior leads to the forfeiture, at least temporarily, of certain rights is embedded in the practice of every legal system known to me. Law enforcement officers are allowed to behave toward those believed to have committed crimes in ways that would not be permitted in different circumstances, and convicted criminals are deprived of rights that we would otherwise consider essential. Yet the idea that "guilty" and "innocent" persons have different degrees of dignity is directly contrary to the idea of dignity as an inalienable characteristic inherent in all human beings. So perhaps the criminals who are subject to the *finaler Rettungsschuss* and the hypothetical hijackers forfeit, but their dignity-derived right to life. In which case we are returned to the situation in which someone may forfeit their right to life but not their right not to be depicted as a copulating pig.

All in all then, I find the Court's claim that it has consistently interpreted dignity as an inner kernel of human value that may never be compromised or balanced hard to sustain.

In the last chapter I identified four strands in the conceptual make-up of dignity. The first was dignity as a rank or status—and human dignity as the status or rank proper to human beings just as human beings. The second was that of intrinsic value: something that, according to Kant, only human beings (strictly speaking, the moral law within them) have. The third was dignity as measured and self-possessed behavior. Fourthly, there was the idea that people should be treated *with* dignity—that is, respectfully. In this connection, we should remind ourselves that there is a crucial distinction between respecting dignity by fulfilling the claims that it makes ("respect as observance") and respecting dignity by showing respect to the person who embodies it ("respect as respectfulness"). The practice of the German courts illustrates how consequential the failure to differentiate these separate strands can be.

Officially, the fundamental idea motivating the use of dignity in the Grundgesetz is the second strand—dignity as intrinsic value. This conception of dignity is asserted to be inviolable and to be the source of deontological claims. The abortion decisions show the German courts appealing to this second strand as the ground for what is arguably the most fundamental human right—the right to life. The idea of dignity is assumed to underpin the claim of the fetus's right to life, and observing that right is what counts as respecting the fetus's dignity. No argument is presented to explain the connection between human dignity and the right to life, but perhaps in this case none is needed. Who, after all, would deny that human beings have a right to life and that that flows from whatever it is that gives human beings their intrinsic value?

Yet the German courts have often operated on the assumption that violations of dignity involve treatment that is in some way demeaning or degrading (as, for example, in the depiction of Franz-Josef Strauss as a copulating pig). The Verfassungsgericht articulated this doc-

~~~e as a matter of explicit principle in a judgment of

~o-called Abhörurteil:

~gs are frequently objects—not just

~ances and of social developments,

but also of the law, insofar as they must obey it without regard to their own interests. This is not sufficient for a violation of human dignity. It must also be the case that they are subjected to treatment that fundamentally calls into question their quality as subjects, or that treatment in a particular case contains arbitrary contempt for the dignity of the human being. Thus the treatment of human beings by public authority charged with executing the law, if it is to affront human dignity, must be an expression of contempt for the value that the human being has in virtue of being a person; it must, in this sense, be "disrespectful treatment." (BVerfGE, 30, 1)

The move from the idea of human dignity as a central core of intrinsic value that acts as the foundation for rights claims in general (the second strand in the meaning of dignity) to the idea of dignity as the prohibition of certain kinds of degrading and disrespectful treatment (the fourth strand) certainly makes things clearer in some ways. It seems simpler to establish what counts as degrading and disrespectful treatment than to decide what rights follow from the possession of dignity conceived as the kernel of human value. Nevertheless, this transition between meanings is obviously highly problematic. Dignity is represented as the value underlying the Grundgesetz's claim to protect fundamental human rights by judicial review, while, according to this doctrine, its scope is stricted by the idea that violations of dignity involve the expression of disrespect. How do the two go together? Two members of the Verfassungsgericht (Judges von Schlabrendorff and Rupp) deciding the Abhörurteil put the point I am making here in a dissenting opinion. One must not restrict the interpretation of the dignity clause of the constitution, they wrote, to "contemptuous treatment"— actions that express contempt for the value that human beings have in virtue of their personhood. In that case, the force of the dignity provisions of the Grundgesetz "would be reduced to the prohibition of the re-introduction of torture, the pillory and the methods of the Third Reich. Such a restriction would not do justice to the conception and spirit of the Grundgesetz" (BVerfGE, 30, 1).

Which is not to say, of course, that dignity as the expression of respect is not important. But it is not plausible, surely, to think that all of the fundamental human rights that we should look to courts to protect against the incursions of the state involve this kind of disrespectfulness. The Abhörurteil itself illustrates the danger. The court's requirement that violations of dignity express contempt for the value of personhood was articulated as part of a judgment in which the court refused to review whether laws that permitted the state to engage in surveillance and interception of mail and telephone communications were in violation of human dignity. In this case, the court—while asserting that dignity is the general principle that guides the law in setting limits to state power—used the restriction of dignity as a reason for refusing even to consider a very significant intrusion into the citizen's private realm as a possible infraction of dignity.

The identification of the violation of dignity with degrading treatment is present in the Air Safety Law judgment. The passengers and crew are said to be being treated as means but also to be being "objectified" *(verdinglicht)* by the shooting down of their plane. In Kant's philosophy, however, the principle that humanity is always to be treated as an end and never as a means only is not restricted to overtly disrespectful treatment. Making a promise while not intending to keep it or giving oneself up to a life of self-indulgent pleasure are, for Kant, just as much ways of treating "humanity" as "a means only" as torture would be. The interpretation of the idea that we may not treat people as "means only" that is dominant among Kant interpreters in the English-speaking world reflects this and makes it a matter, not of the expression of disrespect, but of their being treated in ways to which they could not consent. As Christine Korsgaard puts it: "The question whether another can assent to your way of acting can serve as a criterion for judging whether you are treating her as a mere means."

How would this apply to the case of a hijacked airliner? What could the passengers and crew consent to? Of course, in the circumstances it would not be physically possible for passengers and crew to consent or dissent at all. But is it not overwhelmingly likely that, if they were given the opportunity to express their will, they would choose to die immediately by being shot down with their captors, rather than an hour or so later while being used as part of a missile aimed at their fellow citizens? In their dreadful predicament, they have no way to avoid being treated as means. Even if the state is using them as a means to a further end (to protect other potential victims), so, to no lesser degree, are the hijackers—and their ends are monstrous ones. If, by their deaths, the passengers and crew would be saving the lives of other innocent people, would that not in fact redeem them from being used as "means only"? We need only recall the heroism of the passengers on United Airlines Flight 93 who prevented their flight's hijackers from carrying out their wicked goal by wresting back the controls from them and causing their plane to crash in a field to see that the passengers might well consent rationally to being treated in that way. Would any group of innocent people caught in such an awful situation not want the same? Yet the Verfassungsgericht did not even consider possible consent by the passengers and crew as a criterion in assessing the rightness or wrongness of the Air Safety Law. This failure may be partly a result of the identification of violations of dignity with actively disrespectful treatment, but it is also, I think, part of a more basic tendency in German jurisprudence to give little weight to consent in the consideration of dignity.

VIII. Voluntarism

In May 2008 the Harvard professor of psychology, Steven Pinker, published an article in the *New Republic* with the combative title "The Stupidity of Dignity." Pinker there associated himself with the views of Ruth Macklin, which he summarizes as follows:

> The problem is that "dignity" is a squishy, subjective notion, hardly up to the heavyweight moral demands assigned to it. The bioethicist Ruth Macklin, who had been fed up with loose talk about dignity intended to squelch research and therapy, threw down the gauntlet in a 2003 editorial, "Dignity Is a Useless Concept." Macklin argued that bioethics has done just fine with the principle of personal autonomy—the idea that, because all humans have the same minimum capacity to suffer, prosper, reason, and choose, no human has the right to impinge on the life, body, or freedom of another. This is why informed consent serves as the bedrock of ethical research and practice, and it clearly rules out the kinds of abuses that led to the birth of bioethics in the first place, such as Mengele's sadistic pseudoexperiments in Nazi Germany and the withholding of treatment to indigent black patients in the infamous Tuskegee syphilis study. Once you recognize the principle of autonomy, Macklin argued, "dignity" adds nothing.

In short, dignity amounts to "autonomy" and autonomy protects our "life, body, and freedom."

The Catholic view is evidently sharply different. As we saw, *Veritatis Splendor* takes issue with what the Pope identifies as the modern tendency to "exalt" freedom into an "absolute." For the Catholic Church, autonomy, in the sense of human beings' right to choose for themselves how to live, is not the same as dignity and is, in fact, a value subordinate to it. Hence, on the Catholic view, informed consent cannot be, as Pinker says, "the bedrock" of medical ethics: dignity can act as a ground for overriding the choices of individuals.

The depth of the disagreement between those who identify dignity with autonomy, like Pinker and Macklin, and the Catholic ethical view is apparent when we consider the phrase "death with dignity." The third strand of dignity distinguished in the previous chapter (as we saw in the case of Winckelmann and Schiller) connects dignity with the capacity to endure suffering without loss of self-control. Grave illness threatens human beings' capacity for self-control, and the slogan "death with dignity" expresses the claim that autonomy gives human beings the right to choose to remove themselves from such a state before their dignity in this sense disappears. Catholics will agree with liberals that the dying are entitled to be treated *with dignity* (that is, to be treated with appropriate respectfulness—the fourth strand of dignity's meaning) but they reject the claim that human dignity (in the sense of human beings' intrinsic value) entitles them to choose whether to live or die. The Catechism of the Catholic Church makes it very clear that, on the Catholic view, human beings have no right to choose to end their own lives:

> Everyone is responsible for his life before God who has given it to him. It is God who remains the sovereign Master of life. We are obliged to

accept life gratefully and preserve it for his
honor and the salvation of our souls. We are
stewards, not owners, of the life God has en-
trusted to us. It is not ours to dispose of.

Clearly, this is a substantive ethical dispute involving
different senses of dignity, not one to be settled by appealing to the true meaning (or meaninglessness) of "dignity."
One may, of course, disagree with the Catholic use of the
term, but it has at least as much semantic pedigree behind it as the equation of dignity with autonomy, and it is
wrong (and not particularly clever) to call it "stupid."

As it happens, Kant himself comes down strongly on
the Catholic side of this question. As was noted in the previous chapter, "autonomy," for Kant, means that the moral
law to which human beings are subject is "self-given," not
that human beings have a sovereign power to dispose of
their lives as they wish. Human beings must see themselves as the bearers of something that goes beyond their
exercise of the power of choice, and this aspect of their
selves must be honored and respected under all circumstances. "Personhood"—"humanity in one's person"—is the
ground of duties to oneself. "Humanity in my person" sets
limits to what human beings may choose—even if those
choices are mutually consistent and do not interfere with
the free choices of others. Many of Kant's modern advocates (particularly in the English-speaking world) present
Kant as a "voluntarist"—that is, they take Kant to see the
ultimate source of value in (as Korsgaard puts it) "the
power to set an end . . . and pursue it by rational means."

Nevertheless, as we can see from the following quotation, "humanity in my person," for Kant, is prior to the power of choice and overrides it:

> Personhood, or humanity in my person, is conceived as an intelligible substance, the seat of all concepts, that which distinguishes man in his freedom from all objects under whose jurisdiction he stands in his visible nature.... There is thus lodged in man an unlimited capacity that can be determined to operate in his nature through himself alone and not through anything else in nature. This is freedom, and through it we may recognize the duty of self-preservation. (*Ak.* 27:627–628)

Kant, like the Catholics, regards human beings as stewards, not owners, of the intrinsic value they carry in themselves. Hence, suicide is always a crime—a violation of one's duty to oneself:

> A man can indeed dispose over his condition, but not over his person, for he himself is an end and not a means. (*Ak.* 27:343)

Modern liberals, on the other hand, endorse the principle that human beings—adult and rational ones, at least—have the right to decide for themselves how to live their lives, whether because they believe in John Stuart Mill's "principle of liberty" ("the only purpose for which power can be rightfully exercised over any member of a civilized community, against his will, is to prevent harm

to others") or in the libertarian doctrine that human beings own themselves. The liberty principle is conspicu-
ously absent from the interpretation of dignity as it appears in the German Grundgesetz, and behind Pinker's
hostility to "dignity" is, I think, the suspicion that the
attempt by religious thinkers to import "dignity" into
moral and legal discourse in the USA is a cover for efforts
to abridge that principle. This would certainly be a significant change. Twenty years ago, the Supreme Court
articulated an interpretation of dignity that ties dignity
to autonomy and the liberty principle. In *Planned Parent-
hood of Southeastern Pa. v. Casey,* the Supreme Court revisited the question of abortion that it had addressed in the
famous case of *Roe v. Wade,* with the object of enunciat-
ing more coherently the principles behind that judgment.
In the majority opinion, the Court stated :

> These matters, involving the most intimate
> and personal choices a person may make in a
> lifetime, *choices central to personal dignity and au-
> tonomy,* are central to the liberty protected by
> the Fourteenth Amendment. *At the heart of lib-
> erty is the right to define one's own concept of exis-
> tence, of meaning, of the universe, and of the mystery
> of human life.* Beliefs about these matters could
> not define the attributes of personhood were
> they formed under compulsion of the State.
> (505 U. S. 833 [1992], my emphasis)

Something similar had been expressed earlier. In *Cohen v.
California* the Court asserted that the First Amendment

guarantee of free speech derived from "the belief that no other approach would comport with the premise of individual dignity and choice upon which our political system rests" (403 U.S. 15, 24 [1971]). Consistently with this, at much the same time as the Verfassungsgericht upheld the conviction of the publishers of the Strauss caricature, a very similar case in the USA was being decided quite differently. In 1988 the Supreme Court decided unanimously that a parody advertisement in *Hustler* magazine, in which the Protestant minister Jerry Falwell was described as having incestuous sex with his mother, was protected under the First Amendment, even though the representation was intended to cause emotional distress (*Hustler Magazine, Inc. v. Falwell*, 485 U.S. 46 [1988]). In short, dignity—so far, at least—has been used in American jurisprudence to defend the right to express oneself disrespectfully as an essential matter of individual choice, not to represent the victims of disrespectful speech as suffering a violation of an essential core of the self.

IX. Conclusion

We have come a long way from Morsang-sur-Orge. We started with a French law in which the protection of dignity was made part of public order and involved the state prohibiting behavior that was freely chosen and took place in private. Using the value of dignity to override individuals' freedom to behave as they please might make sense if what were being protected was indeed "respect for the dignity of the human person," but in this case the state was enforcing on individuals the duty of dignified behavior. The German Grundgesetz establishes the Catholic or Kantian conception of dignity as an essential value as the central principle guiding state action. The problem here, however, as we saw, was that it is not clear how this essential value functions as the ground of rights—and what rights does it ground? For Catholicism, human dignity gives life a value that may properly override the choices made by the individual living it. On the other hand, for liberals in the United States in particular, dignity is identified with autonomy in the sense of individuals' right to choose for themselves how to live (and die). Moreover, given that even supposedly basic rights (such as the right to life) come into conflict with one another, how can one maintain that dignity is "inviolable"? The difficulty of sustaining this doctrine appears to be at least part of the reason for the German courts moving toward a more restricted interpretation of dignity, by which violations of dignity are expressive of disrespect. Thus the Kantian idea that we should treat people always as ends and never as means only is interpreted not as a general test for moral behavior based on what human beings could consent to but as a rule that is infringed only when a certain kind of contempt is displayed.

Focusing attention on the fourth strand in the understanding of dignity emphasizes the value of the symbolic or expressive aspects of our behavior toward others. Treating people correctly is both a matter of what we do and of how (that is to say, with what attitudes) we do it. Frequently it is hard to disentangle these two aspects of an action, and, arguably, in many cases it is also unnecessary. In risking my life to pull a drowning man to safety, it is, surely, not necessary to give further expression to my attitude toward him. In setting my life at risk, I am putting beyond doubt my acknowledgment of the value of his humanity. The issue becomes clearer, however, when we think of cases where we consider it right to treat people in ways that go drastically against the ways in which they themselves wish to be treated—when we fight against them in war, for example, or punish them as part of the criminal justice system. Here it is of great importance that we act in ways that express—perhaps to them and perhaps to others—that they are acknowledged as having the entitlement to be treated with respect. We may (under certain circumstances) fight our enemies, but we may not humiliate them; we may punish criminals but we must not degrade them. What *counts* as humiliating or degrading treatment varies drastically from culture to culture, but that is no reason for relativism: the idea that humiliation or degradation counts as a violation of human dignity has a very good claim to be universal even though the practices by which that may be expressed vary. Nevertheless, this conception of dignity, important though it is, is not equivalent to the idea of dignity as the central core of value behind human rights in general. It is indeed a bad thing to add "insult to injury" but we should not mistake the insult for the injury itself.

To close this chapter, however, I want to raise a puzzling question. I have suggested that we have an expressive or symbolic duty to acknowledge human beings as

worthy of respect and that this is a plausible interpretation of the idea that dignity embodies a claim beyond the
general claims that human beings have on one another
in virtue of the intrinsic value of their personhood. But
do we owe such duties only to persons? It is a violation of
dignity to torture and degrade our enemies while they
are alive. But what about when they are dead? Do we not
also violate their dignity if, for example, we leave their
bodies unburied to be eaten by animals? In my opinion,
the answer to this question is definitely yes. But, in that
case, to whom do we owe this duty? *Whose* dignity is violated? The answer to this question will be the focus of
the next chapter.

3

DUTY TO HUMANITY

I. Humanism

To respect someone's dignity requires that one treats them "with dignity"—that is, they must not be treated in ways that degrade, insult, or express contempt. But it is not only living human beings whom we believe deserve to be treated with respect: we are required to dispose of human remains according to prescribed rituals. The precise content of such rituals varies widely—should corpses be buried, burned, or left to be eaten by vultures?—but their existence and, as it seems, symbolic force, is strikingly general. At the end of the previous chapter I said that, in my opinion, the universally held belief that we have a duty to treat dead bodies with respect represents a deep puzzle for moral philosophy. Why it is a puzzle and how that puzzle should be resolved will be the subject of this chapter. To introduce it, I need to take a step back and ask an extremely general question about moral philosophy.

My starting point is the following question. If an action is good, must it be of benefit to someone? The thought that the answer to this must be yes will seem to many—perhaps most—people obvious. After all, if an action is not good for somebody—yourself or somebody else—how could you have a reason to do it? If we make the (important) qualification that the "somebody" in question should be "any morally valuable being" (and may include at least some animals), then the answer "yes" is assumed by utilitarians. All that matters for utilitarians is pleasure and pain, and it is only certain beings that have that capacity. So an action that has no positive impact on pleasure and pain—whether immediately or indirectly—falls outside the scope of morality for the utilitarian.

The position I am describing corresponds to what Joseph Raz (in his book *The Morality of Freedom*) calls "humanism." Raz writes:

> To simplify discussion I will endorse right away the humanistic principle which claims that the explanation and justification of the goodness or badness of anything derives ultimately from its contribution, actual or possible, to human life and its quality.

This is a perfect illustration of the point about philosophy that I made in the Preface. To follow Raz, the humanistic principle does not need arguing for: it is something to "endorse right away" in order to "simplify discussion." And, of course, some things *do* have to be taken for granted for discussion to get going at all. Yet, since Socrates at least, philosophers have seen it as the glory of their subject to place otherwise unquestioned assumptions under scrutiny. And humanism is, I shall argue, a case in point. ("Humanism" is not an ideal label, both because it is currently used in so many other senses and because many utilitarians give weight to the well-being of animals and humans equally. Since in other respects what I want to discuss is just what Raz describes, I shall use that word here. But please remember that this is a very specific sense of the word and that the beneficiaries in question may well include animals.)

The fact that utilitarianism comes down so heavily on the side of humanism should not make us assume that those who oppose utilitarianism will necessarily give the question a different answer. If we are deontologists and say that it is not always right to maximize the good, despite the greater amount of well-being that could be generated by such actions, then, on its most natural interpretation, we are saying that the interests of one or more individuals—the potential torture victim, for example—should outweigh the competing benefits to other parties. Rights, in Ronald Dworkin's famous phrase, are trumps. So here again the benefit to someone is essential to the goodness (or, as deontologists would prefer, rightness) of the action; the difference is just how different kinds of benefit and benefits to different people should be weighed against one another. For the humanist, whether utilitarian or deontological, the idea that we have a duty to treat a corpse with dignity is obviously problematic, however: whom does it benefit?

II. A Utilitarian Response

Faced with examples of people thinking that they have strong moral reasons to do (or refrain from doing) things that seem to have nothing to do with happiness, utilitarians often tell a sociological or biological story along the following lines. "It is true," they say, "that our tendency to act in certain ways (for instance, to recoil in horror at the thought of a corpse being eaten by animals) is a prejudice with no rational foundation. But human beings are not wholly rational animals—and, from the point of view of happiness, it is no bad thing that they aren't. On the contrary, having all sorts of taboos is a good thing. Squeamishness about the treatment of human bodies is valuable to the extent that it gives an emotional foundation to the limits that society has an interest in placing upon human selfishness and ruthlessness. So, irrational though they are, we should certainly not try to eliminate such prejudices—they are valuable from the point of view of happiness."

Now there are two objections to this kind of argument. First of all, loose pieces of speculative anthropology of this kind—"Just So Stories"—can be introduced for a great deal of human behavior, and there is very little to support them beyond the general idea that deeply entrenched and widely held human attitudes must have some positive, evolutionary rationale.

But what really makes me balk at the idea that our conviction that corpses are to be treated with dignity is just a piece of evolutionarily useful fetishism is the following. If it is a taboo, then it is a taboo that we do not think that we would ever be better off without. I can imagine someone saying, "I only wish I weren't so squeamish at the sight of blood—otherwise I think I would make a good surgeon." To be able to free ourselves from such a taboo would be liberating, even though we can recognize how useful it might be in general that it exists. But I can't imagine thinking the same about the belief that corpses ought to be treated with dignity. On the contrary, I would find someone who lacked that belief to be disturbing, even monstrous. This isn't, of course, the last word on the argument (as I mentioned in the Preface, if you want to defend a philosophical position badly enough, there is almost always some way of doing so), but I shall leave it here and move on to what is, to my mind, a more interesting response that the humanist might make.

III. Externalism

To introduce this response, we must ask a second general question. If an action benefits someone, must it affect their awareness? Not, note, must they be aware *that* they are benefited?, but: must their awareness be altered (positively) in some way as a result of the action by which they are benefited? If some Victorian philanthropist planted a wood that is now appreciated for its peace and wildlife, then he has benefited us by making our lives more enjoyable, even if we aren't aware that he has done so (we might think that the wood had been there since before human civilization). The question is whether someone could be made better or worse off without in some way *feeling* differently. When I say "feeling differently," I mean this both positively and, potentially, negatively. If we save someone from being assaulted without their realizing that they were even liable to be attacked, they are still better off and their awareness has been altered for the better in the sense that they *would* have felt much worse off had they been assaulted.

Many will initially find the connection between being benefited and there being either some positive change in one's awareness (or the prevention of a negative change) obviously true, but it is not so. Consider the following example. A woman has an unfaithful boyfriend. She is not aware of his unfaithfulness; her relationship is no less satisfactory and the attitudes that others take toward her do not change. Is she nevertheless worse off? There is a strong pull, surely, toward the answer "yes." What the woman wants, after all, is a faithful partner, not the belief that she has a faithful partner. Now if (as seems plausible) what makes her better off is having her desires fulfilled, it is, you might think, obvious that she is worse off, since her desire is, in fact, not fulfilled. She wants to have her desire fulfilled—not to think (falsely) that it is fulfilled. Hence, she is worse off, despite not being aware of it. Let me call this position "externalism about well-being." Externalism about well-being is an answer that the humanist can give to the puzzle why we should treat a corpse with dignity. To treat a corpse with dignity is to benefit the person whom the corpse once was, even though (of course) the person themselves, since he or she is now dead, can never know that they have thereby been made better off. If you are attracted to this answer, however, I have a further case for you to consider that you should, I think, still find puzzling.

Accept please, at least for the sake of this argument if you do not do so already, that a fetus at some early stage (say, around week ten) is not yet a person and that, in some circumstances at least, abortion would be permissible. Now consider how that now-dead fetus should be treated. May it be treated any old how? Thrown in a rubbish bin? Flushed down the toilet? My conviction is that it too must be treated with dignity. But why? It is not just that the fetus is not aware that it is being benefited by being treated with dignity; in this case (by assumption) there never was or will be a *person* to be benefited. And yet I still strongly believe that the dead fetus should be treated with dignity. For this reason, I think that the route of "humanism plus externalism-about-well-being" is not the right one to take. It is time to consider the alternative to humanism.

IV. Non-Human Things May Be Intrinsically Good

If it is not true that actions are good because they benefit someone, the alternative would appear to be that good actions are good because they are directed toward things that are good independent of their relationship to sentient beings. Of course, such good things may (indeed, probably, *must*) also be good for sentient beings, but their goodness does not depend on that relation. What sort of things might they be? One familiar answer is the Platonic one: that there exists an ideal realm of what is timelessly good. The Platonic position, however, throws the problem of the beneficial effects of action back in our faces. Things that exist in the ideal realm presumably cannot be affected by human action, from which it follows that they cannot be the goal of human action in the sense of being what we should aim to bring into existence, protect from destruction, or increase the quantity of. By assumption, the Platonic good does not require human beings in order for it to exist. The most that can be required of us is that we should know, love, admire, model ourselves on, or (perhaps) worship that timelessly good thing. For Plato himself, human beings relate to the good principally as knowers: if we know the good, then we will, necessarily, act well, but we will be bringing ourselves thereby into a certain (rational) relation to goodness, not bringing goodness itself into existence or increasing its quantity.

However, it is not necessary to believe in a timeless, Platonic realm to oppose humanism. Another form of anti-humanism asserts that there are some finite things whose existence is good independent of the existence of human beings (or other sentient, morally valuable creatures) and that it is good for human beings to produce or preserve such things. The obvious example of such independently good things, for those who take this view, is beautiful objects. Beautiful objects—whether they be naturally beautiful things or things produced by human activity—are valuable for human beings. But they are valuable (or so it is argued) because human beings are able to perceive the value that is intrinsic in them, not because human beings somehow confer that value on them. Since their value is intrinsic, it is good that they exist and that they should continue to do so independently of any relation that they have to the human beings who may (or, indeed, may not) recognize that value.

G. E. Moore presents this view in his *Principia Ethica*. In a famous passage, he considers the possibility of two different worlds:

> Let us imagine one world exceedingly beautiful. Imagine it as beautiful as you can; put into it whatever on this earth you most admire— mountains, rivers, the sea; trees, and sunsets, stars and moon. Imagine these all combined in the most exquisite proportions, so that no one thing jars against another, but each contributes to the beauty of the whole. And then imagine the ugliest world you can possibly conceive. Imagine it simply one heap of filth, containing everything that is most disgusting to us, for whatever reason, and the whole, as far as may be, without one redeeming feature. . . . The only thing we are not entitled to imagine is that any human being ever has or ever, by any possibility, *can,* live in either, can ever see and enjoy the beauty of the one or hate the foulness of the other. Well, even so, supposing them quite apart from any possible contemplation by human beings; still, is it irrational to hold that it is better that the beautiful world should exist than the one which is ugly? Would it not be well, in any case, to do what we could to produce it rather than the other? Certainly I cannot help thinking that it would; and I hope that some may agree with me in this extreme instance.

Let us continue in Moore's spirit and imagine the end of life in the universe (and assume that there is no divine being to perceive it). Even in that inert, perceptionless world, so we must suppose on this view, it would be better that (say) the ceiling of the Sistine Chapel should survive than that it should crumble to dust with the passing of the last sentient being, even though there will be no eyes any more to see its colors, and preserving it would be a worthy undertaking for the last sentient being to undertake in her final days. As you can tell, I am sure, I do not find this view very plausible, but even if you find it more appealing than I do, I think that it is very doubtful that it can help us to resolve the puzzle with which I started. What good thing would be produced and continue to exist if the last sentient being in the universe were to treat the corpse of the next-to-last one with dignity?

V. Duty

The puzzle of our obligation to treat the dead with dignity is then, I think, truly deep and difficult, and none of the possible positions that I have just proposed appeals to me as offering a plausible resolution of it. Is there some neglected alternative? Indeed, I believe that there is—but it is a position that is currently so unfashionable that I cannot think of any moral philosopher who defends it. Yet it is a position that, I have to say, the more I consider it, the more persuasive I find it. I shall spend the rest of this chapter trying to persuade you to share my conviction.

As explained in the previous chapter, contemporary philosophers, following Rawls, standardly divide moral theories into two camps, the teleological and the deontological, according to whether the right is interpreted as being a matter of maximizing the good or not. Rights-based theories are paradigmatic deontological theories (to have a right, on this view, means precisely that there are times when it is right to do something—respect the right in question—even though to do so does not maximize the good) while utilitarianism is the paradigmatic teleological theory. Rights (if they are "claim rights" and not mere permissions) lay duties on other people, and it seems natural from the humanistic perspective that, if we have duties, then they must be duties to benefit some morally valuable being. Seen in this way, rights-based theories are, like utilitarianism, humanistic in the sense defined earlier.

Etymologically, however, a "deontology" is a doctrine of duties, and there is, in fact, a distinction of principle between duty-based theories and rights-based ones. Could we have duties with no corresponding beneficiaries? Onora O'Neill has argued for the existence of duties without rights. Her example is the duty to give to charity, which, she says very plausibly, may still be a duty even though no specific individual has the right to receive the benefit of charity. Clearly, however, O'Neill's example remains within the orbit of humanism: there are beneficiaries to the duty of charity, even if the latter are not *entitled* to those benefits as a matter of right. The position that I am proposing is far more radical: that we have a duty to treat a corpse with dignity just because one of the ways in which we have a duty to act is that we should perform acts that are expressive of our respect. This is not a duty that we owe either to any particular being or agent who will be benefited by our performance of it or even one that we owe to humanity as a whole, viewed as collective beneficiaries. To explore such a duty-based approach to morality, let us map it onto the questions asked earlier.

Most fundamentally, the duty-based approach to morality I am advocating is not committed to humanism. Thus, we may have a duty to act in a way that does not benefit another intrinsically valuable being—not even ourselves. (Here is the difference between a duty-based theory and the currently fashionable approach to morality called "virtue ethics." For virtue ethics—so far as I can make it out—acting well benefits the virtuous agent because it is part of living a good life—the "good life" being understood as good not in the sense of being pleasurable but in some more refined, neo-Aristotelian way, as promoting the agent's *"eudaimonia,"* her "flourishing." So virtue ethics is a kind of humanism with an enlarged idea of what human well-being amounts to.) Hence, a duty-based theorist may remain agnostic whether there must be a connection with the awareness of the being who is benefited for that being to be made better off by an action. Finally, the duty-based theorist does not have to believe that, in doing his or her duty, an agent is bringing into being, preserving, or otherwise relating to something whose existence is intrinsically valuable independently of its relationship to human beings (although, as we shall see, Kant, in fact, does think just that).

The idea that duty should have primacy is hardly considered in contemporary moral philosophy, because, I assume, the idea that duties should have force absent a morally significant beneficiary seems simply too bizarre for contemporary moral philosophers to take seriously. Something like it can be found in the literature on so-called "agent-relative reasons" in the idea that there are certain actions that are incumbent on the agent (or certain actions that are prohibited) because of who she is. In the most usually given example, it is pointed out that parents have a special duty to look after their children. But here the thought is that certain individuals have particular obligations to do things that benefit other morally valuable beings, although such obligations don't derive from general principles. In other words, they nevertheless remain within the framework of "humanism," as I have called it. My suggestion is different. It is both more radical (we have duties toward corpses, even though no person benefits) and more general (this is something that all of us have just by being human; it is not restricted to people in particular social relations).

I have not hesitated to point out what seem to me to be the objections to alternative approaches to the problem of our duty to treat the dead with dignity, and so it is only fair that I do the same for the duty-based approach. It is certainly strange. I am saying, am I not, that we have the duty to act in ways that express respect—but to whom am I to express that respect? Surely "expression" is a communicative act. Would the last sentient being in the universe still have such a duty, even if there were no one to listen to her? My answer—oddly enough, you might think—is yes. Moreover, I have a duty to express this attitude not just by the way that I behave toward those who paradigmatically embody the value of humanity—live human beings—but toward things that do not: fetuses and corpses. Put this way, duty-based morality sounds like an example of ethics carried out, as Nietzsche would put it, under the shadow of God—even those who, officially, do not believe in God, Nietzsche alleges, still think and act in ways that make sense only on the assumption of the existence of an all-seeing, judging God. If God is not there to hear, why express respect? The duty theorist has, I think, no further reply: he or she must simply appeal to the conviction that, nonetheless, the expression of respect would remain a duty, even if there is no one else to perceive it.

VI. Kant

At this point, I want to make a detour and return for one final time to the interpretation of Kant's moral philosophy. I do so for two reasons. First, by looking at Kant from the perspective of the issues just raised, we shall, I hope, understand better some of the most striking (and, to modern liberals, off-putting) features of his thought about the dignity of humanity. Secondly, we can use Kant to articulate the structure of the duty-based approach to ethics that I am here advocating.

Kant is not, in the Razian sense in which I have been using the term, a humanist. Many of the duties that he considers obligatory for human beings do not benefit anyone by their fulfillment—and in other cases, if they do, it is not in virtue of the fact that they are of benefit that they are obligatory. Nor are our duties derivative from the rights of other morally significant beings. Indeed, Kant believes that our most fundamental duties (including, surprisingly enough, the duty of telling the truth) are duties toward ourselves. Kant is, in the terms used in this chapter, a certain kind of Platonist. That is, he believes that what is intrinsically good is something that is timeless and that right action consists not in trying to bring that timelessly valuable thing into existence or defending it from destruction (which is both impossible and unnecessary) but in acting in ways that are appropriate toward it. For Kant, however (unlike Plato), that intrinsically good thing is not independent of human beings—on the contrary, it exists in them as their inner transcendental kernel.

For Plato, the appropriate stance toward what is intrinsically good is a cognitive one—we should strive to know it. In the end, right action itself is a kind of expression of knowledge. For Kant, what is intrinsically good must be treated in a way that respects the fact of its intrinsic goodness—its dignity. By "respect" here I do not mean respect-as-observance (that we should respect what is good in the way that we respect the speed limit) but that we should adopt an *attitude of respect* toward it and act in ways that are expressive of that attitude. Kant's ethics is an ethics of duty, but it might also be called an ethics of respectfulness, an ethics of honor, or even an ethics of reverence. Its guiding thought is that we have a duty to act in ways that are both respectful and worthy of respect.

What is this timeless object that is intrinsically valuable for Kant? The answer was given clearly enough in the *Groundwork:* "morality, and humanity insofar as it is capable of morality, is that which alone has dignity" (*Ak.* 4:435). Morality, says Kant, has dignity—not because it brings about something good but in itself. We may follow morality or not, but morality itself is not something that we can bring into being or destroy. It is natural to think that when Kant says that humanity has dignity he means that the object of moral life should be to act in ways that benefit human beings. But this interpretation is wrong. As Kant makes clear, in his view morality does not take its value from what it contributes to humanity; humanity has value in virtue of being capable of morality. In one of the most celebrated passages in the *Critique of Practical Reason,* Kant asks what is the origin of duty ("Sublime and mighty name . . . descent from which is the indispensable condition of that worth which human beings alone can give themselves"; *Ak.* 5:86). His answer is that the intrinsic worth of human beings derives from moral duty and connects human beings to "an order of things that only the understanding can think":

> [The origin of duty] is nothing other than *personhood* [*Persönlichkeit*], that is, freedom and independence from the mechanisms of the whole of nature, regarded nevertheless as also a capacity of a being subject to special laws—namely pure practical laws given by his own reason, so

that a person as belonging to the sensible world
is subject to his own personhood insofar as he
also belongs to the intelligible world; for, it is
then not to be wondered at that a human being,
as belonging to both worlds, must regard his
own nature in reference to his second and highest vocation only with reverence and its laws
with the highest respect. (*Ak.* 5:86–87, translation modified)

The "order of things" to which Kant is here referring is,
of course, his famous "noumenal realm," the "intelligible
world" in which we can be thought to exist as free beings.
Labeling Kant a "Platonist" emphasizes this metaphysical
aspect of Kant's ethical thought that most contemporary
admirers of Kant try to find ways of deflating or working
their way around. Yet perhaps the contrast will turn out to
be less dramatic in practice than the label I have chosen
suggests. On the "voluntarist" reading of Kant that we find
in the writings of Christine Korsgaard, among many others, rational agency is the source of value. The "Platonist"
interpretation of Kant, as I am calling it, also identifies
what is intrinsically valuable with the rational will. If there
were no rational agents in the universe, on this reading,
there would exist nothing that had intrinsic value. So, you
might think, rhetoric apart, the difference between the
two ways of interpreting Kant may not be all that great
after all.

What matters, in the end, is how we move from the
"dignity" of human moral agency as unconditional, inner value to an understanding of what we ought to do,

and here, it seems to me, there really is a deep difference of interpretation. On the voluntarist reading of Kant, the claim is that, for Kant, human willing creates value, provided that that willing is rational. The problem, of course, is to specify what "rational" means. It is a matter of testing actions (to be textually precise, the maxims under which actions are performed) for contradiction. What would happen if these maxims were universalized? Over the years, there have been hundreds and hundreds of interpretations of Kant along these lines, each with its own particular strengths and weaknesses, but the common problem that all of them face, it seems to me, is this: it is very hard to see how many of the actions that Kant claims are prohibited or mandatory truly lead to contradictions if universalized (or universally omitted). This is particularly true of those duties that Kant describes as duties to ourselves. To take one of Kant's own examples, where is the contradiction in saying that human beings may choose to end their own lives if they reach a point at which their suffering is such that they can no longer exercise rational self-control?

Korsgaard is admirably candid about the difficulty of extending the universalizability-test approach she favors to Kant's claim that suicide is a fundamental violation of duty. What the universalizability test asks, according to Korsgaard, is whether, should everyone with the same motive or purpose act in the proposed way, they could still achieve that purpose. But there is, she concedes, "simply no argument to show that everyone suffering from acute misery could not commit suicide and still achieve their purpose: ending that misery." The difficulty that Kantianism faces is not surprising, according to Korsgaard, given that such cases lie at some distance from the basic concerns that the theory is directed toward addressing:

> The kind of case around which the view is framed, and which it handles best, is the temptation to make oneself an exception: selfishness, meanness, advantage-taking, and disregard for the rights of others. It is this sort of thing, not violent crimes born of despair or illness, that serves as Kant's model of immoral conduct. I do not think we can fault him on this, for this and not the other is the sort of evil that most people are tempted by in their everyday lives.

While I can understand why Korsgaard reads Kant in this way, I think just the opposite. In my opinion, cases like that of the prohibition of suicide are central, not peripheral. Kant's moral philosophy is not just directed to "what we owe to each other" but even more so to what we owe to ourselves. So, instead of starting from the question what maxims can be universalized without contradiction, it would be better to understand Kant as asking first how we have to act in order to treat our dignity (our inner kernel of intrinsic value) with the proper respect.

Kant himself asserts the primacy of duties to oneself explicitly both in the *Metaphysics of Morals* and in his *Lectures on Ethics*:

So far from these duties being the lowest, they actually take first place, and are the most important duties of all; for even without first explaining what self-regarding duty is, we may ask how, if a man degrades his own person, anything else can be demanded of him? (*Ak.* 27:341; *Moral Philosophy: Collins*)

Self-regarding duties set limits to our freedom, and these limits flow from the need to act in ways that honor our humanity:

The *principium* of the self-regarding duties does not consist in self-favour, but in self-esteem; our actions, that is, must be in keeping with the worth of humanity. . . . All such duties are founded on a certain love of honour consisting in the fact that a man values himself, and in his own eyes is not unworthy that his actions should be in keeping with humanity. To be worthy in his eyes of inner respect, the treasuring of approval, is the essential ingredient of duties to oneself. (*Ak.* 27:347; *Moral Philosophy: Collins*)

Significantly, Kant's vocabulary does not focus here on requirements of universality and consistency in willing— the apparatus of rationality with which Kant's moral philosophy is generally identified nowadays—so much as respect, esteem, and the "love of honor." Failure to honor the inner value that each of us carries within ourselves makes us unworthy of respect. We do not have to bring the dignity of humanity into being or stop it from being destroyed, but we *do* have to find ways of acting that express esteem for it. If we act in ways that express our esteem for the inner value that we carry within ourselves, we are entitled to respect: our own self-respect and the respect of others.

Suicide is therefore a very important issue indeed for Kant, not something off on the fringes of his concern. It is, he says, "the supreme violation of the duties to oneself" (*Ak.* 27:342; *Moral Philosophy: Collins*). But what can be Kant's objection to it, if not that the universalization of the maxim behind it is inconsistent? Defenders of the permissibility of suicide commonly appeal to one (possibly, both) of two principles, each of which Kant rejects. First, she may argue that people have a right to end their own lives, should they so wish, in virtue of their own "self-ownership." (*Whose Life Is It Anyway?*, to echo the title of a rightly admired play about euthanasia.) Kant (like the Catholic Church) strongly disagrees. "Humanity in our person" prevents us from owning ourselves in the way that we might own a material object, he says, and likewise forbids us from making use of our bodies as things:

> He is indeed the *proprietarius* of it, i.e., he governs and rules over it, but as over a person, i.e., insofar as he would dispose over it as a thing, the phenomenon appears restrained by the noumenon. (*Ak.* 27:593; *Moral Philosophy: Vigilantius*)

Secondly, the defender of the permissibility of suicide may appeal to the idea that the possibility of suicide diminishes human suffering. This too Kant rejects. The argument that someone may, by committing suicide, escape from suffering, reduces our duty to the humanity in our person to a matter of "inclination" or "prudence" [*Klugheit*] when, in fact, it is a matter of acting in such a way that we do honor to it. "Nobody is harmed," he admits, by violations of duties to oneself, "yet it is a dishonoring of the worth of humanity in one's own person":

> Self-regarding duties . . . are independent of all advantage, and pertain only to the worth of being human. They rest on the fact that in regard to our person we have no untrammeled freedom, that humanity in our person must be highly esteemed, since, without this, man is an object of contempt, which is an absolute fault, since he is worthless, not only in the eyes of others, but also in himself. The self-regarding duties are the supreme condition and *principium* of all morality, for the worth of the person constitutes moral worth. (*Ak.* 27:343; *Moral Philosophy: Collins*)

In this and several other similar passages it is clearly apparent that Kant is no humanist. We are the embodiments of a transcendent value—humanity in our persons—and this requires that we act in ways that are respectful of that value, even though there will be no advantage for us or for others in doing so. Suicide is an action that is "contrary to the concept of the right of humanity in my own person; and humanity is in itself an inviolable holiness, wherein my *personhood (Persönlichkeit),* or the right of humanity in my person, is no less inviolably constrained" (*Ak.* 27:627; *Moral Philosophy: Vigilantius*). Hence, we may not dispose of our own lives, despite having overwhelmingly strong material or psychological reasons to want to do so.

Korsgaard, however, offers a different argument on Kant's behalf:

> However obvious it may seem that a "tolerable condition" is a good thing, it is good only because of the value conferred upon it by the choice of a rational being. Destroy the rational being, and you cut off the source of the goodness of this end—it is no longer really an end at all, and it is no longer rational to pursue it.

The weakness in this argument reveals a fundamental problem with the voluntarist interpretation of Kant. If value is really conferred by "the choice of a rational being," as Korsgaard says, what about the value of that choosing being itself? Where does that come from? Either a rational being must have value because of its own choice (which looks like a vicious circle) or there must be at least one thing whose value does not come from the choice of a rational being. Contrast this with the reading of Kant that I have just been developing. On this view, the choices of rational agents have value (when they do—which is not always) because rational agents have value in themselves; they do not derive that value from choices that they make. If Korsgaard is right, then, for Kant the contradiction in suicide is that, in ending one's life, one is destroying the "rational being" that is the source of the goodness of particular ends. Yet I think that we can establish quite clearly from the texts that this is not Kant's view. What has intrinsic, absolute value, for Kant, is not our *lives* but our personhood—"humanity in our persons"—and (odd though it may sound to us today) our personhood and our lives are not the same thing. For that reason, as Kant makes clear in his *Lectures on Ethics,* "in and for itself, life is in no way highly to be prized, and I should seek to preserve my life only insofar as I am worthy to live" (*Ak.* 27:341; *Moral Philosophy: Collins*). In some circumstances the honor due to "humanity in our person" will, in fact, require us to give up our lives:

> Humanity in our person is an object of the highest respect and never to be violated in us. In the cases where a man is liable to dishonor, he is duty bound to give up his life, rather than dishonor the humanity in his own person. For does he do honor to it, if it is to be dishonored by others? If a man can preserve his life in no other way than by dishonoring his humanity, he ought rather to sacrifice it. He then, indeed, puts his animal life in danger, yet he feels that, so long as he has lived, he has lived honorably. It matters not that a man lives long (for it is not his life that he loses by the event, but only the prolongation of the years of his life, since nature has already decreed that he will some day die); what matters is that, so long as he

lives, he should live honorably, and not dishonor the dignity of humanity. If he can now no longer live in that fashion, he cannot live at all; his moral life is then at an end. But moral life is at an end if it no longer accords with the dignity of humanity. (*Ak.* 27:377; *Moral Philosophy: Collins*)

Since a person, for Kant, is not to be identified with her physical existence, what is wrong with suicide cannot be that by ending our lives we "destroy the rational being." It is prohibited, rather, because it is dishonorable: that is, it fails to honor humanity in our persons.

To summarize: the basic starting point of Kant's vision of morality is that we carry within ourselves something of "unconditional, incomparable" value—"personhood" or the "dignity of humanity." Although this value must be treated as an "end" and not as a means, it cannot be increased by human action or function as a goal to be realized by us. Since it is not identified with our "animal life," nor is it something that we have to protect from physical destruction—on the contrary, it may require us to sacrifice our lives. So the dignity of humanity can act as a guide for our behavior only less directly: it requires that we behave in ways that "honor" or "respect" humanity in our person. Although "humanity in our persons" is not itself an end to be pursued or promoted, respecting it does require us, Kant tells us, to pursue certain ends—"one's own perfection and the happiness of others" (*Ak.* 6:385; *The Metaphysics of Morals*)—and to follow certain, allegedly natural, purposes (not to use one's sexual powers "unnaturally," to give a notorious example—*Ak.* 6:424–426; *The Metaphysics of Morals*). Of course, we are also required to act on principles that can be appropriately universalized, principles that will certainly prohibit "selfishness, meanness, advantage-taking, and disregard for the rights of others." But I disagree with Korsgaard that it is this kind of self-seeking behavior that acts as "Kant's model of immoral conduct." On the contrary, such duties should be understood as arising for Kant in the context of other, even more fundamental requirements.

A thought that may well have been going through your mind as I laid out my interpretation of Kant now needs to be addressed. Let us say that you have (as I hope) found that interpretation convincing as a way of understanding the texts. But have I done Kant (or you, if you feel sympathetic to Kant's moral philosophy) any favors by this interpretation? I have, for example, argued that, for Kant, the dignity of humanity is connected with our membership of the noumenal realm, in virtue of which we may see ourselves as embodying a timeless, intrinsic value. From the need to act in ways that are appropriate to that value, Kant purports to draw a number of practical conclusions. What is disturbing is not just that many of these conclusions are out of line with what most people (myself included) would now think is morally required (it is not just lying and suicide that are allegedly prohibited—so, among other things, are homosexuality and masturbation). More worrying for many of those sympathetic to Kant's enterprise will be the fact that Kant's moral philosophy comes out looking far less clear-cut than it is usually thought to be. If the standard is simply that we should act in ways that "respect" or "honor" a fundamental value, how can we argue rationally for or against a particular claim? There is, on my interpretation, no clear test or set of criteria that leads from fundamental value to appropriate action—something to compete with the simple maximizing principle of the utilitarians.

Kant's ethics is not humanistic in the sense used in this chapter because observing our duty cannot benefit the timelessly valuable thing toward which it is directed (although it may, of course, benefit the individuals in whom it is embodied). The existence of this value is connected by Kant with his most ambitious metaphysical claim—that human beings, in virtue of their capacity for free action, are members of a "noumenal" realm beyond the empirical world of appearances. So it is not surprising that Kant's modern-day secular admirers should downplay this connection and interpret it in ways that are less philosophically alarming.

A great revolution took place in moral philosophy during the eighteenth and nineteenth centuries. They saw the development of comprehensive moral systems that did not make reference to a creator-God, either directly, by claims about God's will, or indirectly, by reference to the purposes (allegedly) apparent in God's creation. This is not to say that the advocates of such systems were all unbelievers, just that they aimed to separate morality from religion. One leading approach of this kind that is with us today is, clearly, utilitarianism; and Kantianism, or so it is commonly thought, is the other. Certainly, Kant makes morality independent of belief in God or a teleological view of nature, yet, to follow the interpretation given here, Kant's moral philosophy, with its emphasis on the "inviolable holiness" of humanity and the primacy of respect (the Kantian term *Achtung* is usually translated as "respect" but it would be better perhaps to render it as "reverence") for humanity in our persons turns out to be far from fully secular.

VII. Duty without Platonism

For the religious believer, we owe reverence toward God and, by extension, to those things that we can see as embodying God's will. Yet, absent God, is there any place for reverence at all—let alone at the center of a secular moral system? My claim is that we can reasonably believe that we have a basic duty to respect the dignity of humanity without accepting either humanism (that everything that is good is good only because it benefits a human being) or Platonism (that there are timelessly valuable things toward which we must act with respect or reverence). That is the solution I propose to the puzzle with which I started this chapter.

If we believe for religious reasons that human beings have dignity because they are created in the image of God, or if we believe that they inhabit a realm of noumenal freedom, then there is an objective value that inheres in the targets of our respect, something that serves to pick out human beings from animals or material objects and justify the claims that they make. But do we have to be able to point to such an objective feature for it to be reasonable to think that we have the duty to respect humanity? That we might have such a duty toward things—corpses or fetuses, for example—that are not themselves human and will not benefit from our behavior toward them seems to me persuasive even if we do not think of humanity in Kant's transcendental terms. Such duties are principally symbolic: they require us to act in ways that *express* respect. And I am not put off by the thought that it may well be that we are being asked to express respect when there is no one else there to become aware of that expression. Our duty to respect the dignity of humanity is—on this I agree with Kant—fundamentally a duty toward ourselves. By which I mean, not that we are benefited when we observe our duties, but that our duties are so deep a part of us that we could not be the people that we are without having them. In failing to respect the humanity of others we actually undermine humanity in ourselves.

While my view has a lot in common with Kant's in opposing the apparent commonsense of moral humanism, it is far removed from it in others. Dignity in the sense of being treated with respect for one's humanity is not the fundamental ground of human rights that the Kantian (or Catholic) use of the term would imply. Suffering, to my mind, is bad, and love good, in themselves, not, as Kantianism implies, because of their relationship to something else. Nor are all violations of basic rights symbolic harms, shocking though such violations of dignity may be (remember the shameful pictures from Abu Ghraib prison). When you torture me, you humiliate and degrade me, but the harm is not just that: you cause me extreme pain and thereby deprive me of effective self-control. To do so would be impermissible and would violate a basic human right whether or not it was also associated with an expression of contempt. The worst of what the Nazi state did to the Jews was not the humiliation of herding them into cattle trucks and forcing them to live in conditions of unimaginable squalor; it was to murder them.

Yet this does not mean that dignitary harms are unimportant. To the contrary, as Jonathan Glover documents in his wonderful book, *Humanity: A Moral History of the Twentieth Century*, one of the features that characterized many of the most violent and destructive acts of the twentieth century was the humiliation and symbolic degradation of the victims. It seems to be a deeply rooted part of human nature that human beings are able to engage more easily in the most horrifying behavior toward one another if at the same time they expressively deny the humanity of their victims. One of the facts that Glover points to is that torturers often employ what he calls "cold jokes"—for example, the use of ironically innocuous nicknames for the tools and contexts of their crimes (think of the "Iron Maiden" or the "Romper Room"). This connects back, surely, to Orwell. If humor is "dignity sitting on a tin-tack," then the cold joke is a powerfully effective way of undermining dignity symbolically. And such denials of dignity may clear the psychological pathway to evil. You have all the more reason to be concerned with dignitary harm if, like me, you feel that the barriers that separate the materialistic world of modern liberal democracy from the barbarism and atrocity that disfigured the twentieth century (and show every sign of continuing through the twenty-first) are very, very fragile.

Dignitary harms may also have a material character. One of the key ways in which human dignity is violated is by preventing human beings from behaving in ways that are dignified. Certainly, individuals who are treated in ways that are undignified—say, prisoners who are not allowed to wash or to use proper toilet facilities—may, nevertheless, show great dignity in Schiller's sense by retaining their powers of rationality and self-determination in such degrading circumstances. Nevertheless, the connection remains: part of the point of the degrading treatment was not just to express contempt, but in so doing to undermine the victim's capacity for dignity. That such treatment fails in its objective shows the exceptional degree of self-control—and, hence, dignity—that the victim has.

What expresses contempt for human beings varies, naturally, between cultures and contexts, but there are some striking common themes. Where there are (or were) marked demarcations of social status between human beings, to deprive someone of dignity is, typically, to treat them in a way that attributes to them, expressively or symbolically, a very low social status—they are, literally, *degraded.* Another characteristic demarcation (which goes back, as we have seen, to Cicero's *De Officiis*) is that human dignity is expressed by behavior that marks the distinction between human beings and animals—for example, in upright gait, through the wearing of clothes, in eating subject to a code of table manners, defecating and copulating in private. It is this which the torturers and murderers target. The rhetoric of genocidal propaganda is all too predictable in its denial of the humanity of its victims, from the cartoons of Jews as insects in *Der Stürmer,* to Hutu descriptions of the Tutsi in Rwanda as "cockroaches."

As Schiller recognized, respect for humanity requires us to mark the value of human beings even (or, indeed, especially) when the gross material facts of our animal existence are inescapable—in contexts of death and suffering. So let me close with a famous story about Kant that I find very moving (and inspiring). It was nine days before his death and the great man was old and desperately weak. Nevertheless, he refused to sit down before a guest (his doctor) had first taken a seat. When he was finally persuaded to do so, he said: *"Das Gefühl der Humanität hat mich noch nicht verlassen"* (The feeling of *humanity* has not yet left me).

NOTES

INDEX

NOTES

PREFACE

xiii   *equivalent to proof:* J. S. Mill, *Utilitarianism,* in *On Liberty and Other Essays* (Oxford: Oxford University Press, 2008), p. 135.

1. "THE SHIBBOLETH OF ALL
EMPTY-HEADED MORALISTS"

1   *that expression, dignity of man:* A. Schopenhauer, *On the Basis of Morality* (Indianapolis: Hackett, 1965), p. 100.

2   *the common responsibility of all people:* letter of 28 August 2006, downloaded from http://english.farsnews.net/.

3   *path of dignity:* CBS News, 10 October 2006.

3   *consists of a unique freedom:* R. Niebuhr, *Faith and History* (New York: Scribner's, 1949), p. 124.

3   *The dignity of each and every human being:* J. Moltmann, "Christianity and the Revaluation of the Values of Modernity and of the Western World," in *A Passion for God's Reign* (Grand Rapids, MI: Wm. B. Eerdman's, 1998), p. 34.

3   *David Brooks: New York Times,* 9 July 2009.

4   *popular press:* "Sir Bobby Robson," *The Times* (London), 31 July 2009.

4   *Colonia Dignidad:* Bruce Falconer, "The Torture Colony," *American Scholar,* Autumn 2008.

5   *Dignity is a useless concept:* R. Macklin, "Dignity Is a Useless Concept," *British Medical Journal* (20 December 2003), pp. 1419–1420.

5   *with unnecessary obscurity:* J. Griffin, "A Note on Measuring Well-Being," in *Summary Measures of Population Health,* ed. C. J. L. Murray, p. 131.

5   *potential maker of claims:* J. Feinberg, "The Nature and Value of Rights," reprinted in his *Rights, Justice and the Bounds of Liberty* (Princeton: Princeton University Press, 1980), p. 151.

6   *a virtue:* see A. Kolnai, "Dignity," reprinted in *Dignity, Character and Self-Respect,* ed. R. Dillon (New York: Routledge, 1995), pp. 53–75.

7   *intrinsically disordered: Catechism of the Catholic Church,* 2357.

7   *Gay, Lesbian, Bisexual and Transgender Catholics:* downloaded from DignityUSA.org.

7   *her trampled dignity:* http://www.bbc.co.uk/news/world -latin-america-11480968.

8   *expanding circle narrative:* see, for example, J. Griffin, *On Human Rights* (Oxford: Oxford University Press, 2008), chap. 1; and J. Waldron, *Dignity, Rank and Rights,* The Tanner Lectures on Human Values, Berkeley, 2009 (Oxford: Oxford University Press, forthcoming).

11   *cum dignitate otium:* "Speech on Behalf of Publius Sestius." The phrase also appears in *De Oratore.*

12   *unworthy of the dignity of the human race: De Officiis,* I, 30.

13   *means of your salvation:* Translated in J. H. Robinson, *Readings in European History* (Boston: Ginn, 1905), 72–73

14   *acknowledgment of unworthiness:* J. Ruskin, *The Stones of Venice,* vol. 2: *The Sea Stories* (New York: Cosimo, 2007), p. 159.

15   *by indignities: Essays, Civil and Moral* (Cambridge, MA: Harvard Classics, 1909–1914).

16   *not in necessity: The doctrine & discipline of divorce* (London: [s.n.], 1644), p. 2.

16   *goodness on account of itself: Scriptum super libros Sententiarium,* bk. III, distinction 35, question 1, article 4, solution 1c.

18   *all our dignity consists in thought: Pensées,* 200 (Penguin: Harmondsworth, 1966).

18   *Ig Nobel Prize:* http://improbable.com/ig/winners/#ig2008.

20   *I can turn all things: Von der Freiheit eines Christenmenschens* (1520), 15th thesis.

32   *tranquility in suffering: Über Anmut und Würde* (Stuttgart: Reclam, 1971), p. 121.

33   *fortitude with which the great man endures it:* in *German Aesthetic and Literary Criticism,* ed. H. B. Nisbet (Cambridge: Cambridge University Press, 1985), p. 42.

35   *sublime disposition: Über Anmut und Würde,* p. 113.

35   *morally great:* Ibid., p. 119.

35   *moral freedom of the human being:* Ibid., p. 121.

39   *conformity to his image: Moral Sketches of Prevailing Opinions and Manners, Foreign and Domestic, with Reflections on Prayer* (1820), in *The Works of Hannah More,* vol. 4 (London: T. Cadell, 1830), pp. 370–371.

39   *A black coming in at this moment:* John Bernard, *Retrospections of America, 1797–1811* (1880), pp. 90–91.

41   *history in morality: Deutsch-Brüsseler-Zeitung,* no. 92 (18 November 1847).

42   *serious philosophies and religions:* F. Nietzsche, "The Greek State," in *Early Greek Philosophy and Other Writings,* trans. M. A. Mügge (New York: Russell and Russell, 1964), p. 3.

43   *dignity of labor:* Ibid., pp. 4–5.

43   *preserve his individual existence:* Ibid., p. 5.

44 *crushed by the wheels of the chariot:* Ibid., pp. 7-8.

46 *excuse his existence: the prototype of the state:* Ibid., pp. 16-17.

47 *never either well-trained or accomplished:* A. Tocqueville, *Democracy in America,* vol. 2, trans. Henry Reeve (New York: Colonial Press, 1899), p. 227.

57 *potential maker of claims:* Feinberg, "Nature and Value of Rights," p. 151.

2. THE LEGISLATION OF DIGNITY

64 *absence of particular local circumstances:* Manuel Wackenheim v. France, Communication No. 854/1999, U.N. Doc. CCPR/C/75/D/854/1999 (2002), in United Nations Human Rights Committee, *Selected Decisions under the Optional Protocol, Seventy-Fifth to Eighty-Fourth Sessions* (July 2002–March 2005) (New York: United Nations Publications, 2007), p. 111.

65 *must require the proper respect:* http://www.conseil-etat.fr /cde/fr/presentation-des-grands-arrets/27-octobre-1995 -commune-de-morsang-sur-orge.html.

67 *compatible with the objectives of the Covenant:* Manuel Wackenheim v. France, p. 114.

69 *little people are trying to gain:* Jennifer Brandlon, "Little People," Associated Press, Baltimore, 1 July 1989.

73 *with a bump, is funny:* "Funny but not vulgar," in *The Collected Essays, Journalism and Letters of George Orwell,* vol. 3 (Harmondsworth: Penguin, 1970), p. 325.

78 *justice in the world:* Grundgesetz für die Bundesrepublik Deutschland, 23 May 1949, Article 1.

81 *replaceable magnitude:* Maunz-Dürig, 1958, Art. 1, Abs. 1— see also BVerfGE 45, 187, 227f.

88 *by rational means:* C. Korsgaard, *Creating the Kingdom of Ends* (Cambridge: Cambridge University Press, 1996), p. 124.

89 *could not consent:* O. O'Neill, *Constructions of Reason* (Cambridge: Cambridge University Press, 1989), p. 138.

93   *by rational means:* Korsgaard, *Creating the Kingdom of Ends,*
       p. 124.

103   *an average of ten European countries:* "European Values," TNS-
       Sofres, May 2005, http://www.thebrusselsconnection.be/tbc
       /upload/attachments/European%20Values%20Overall
       %20EN.pdf.

118   *as a mere means:* Korsgaard, *Creating the Kingdom of Ends,*
       p. 139.

120   *adds nothing:* "The Stupidity of Dignity," *New Republic,* 28
       May 2008.

122   *to dispose of:* Catechism of the Catholic Church (Vatican City:
       Libreria Editrice Vaticana, 1993), 2280.

122   *by rational means:* Korsgaard, *Creating the Kingdom of Ends,*
       p. 124.

124   *harm to others:* John Stuart Mill, *On Liberty,* chap. 1.

3. DUTY TO HUMANITY

130   *and its quality: The Morality of Freedom* (Oxford: Oxford
       University Press, 1986), p. 194.

137   *extreme instance: Principia Ethica* (1903) (Cambridge: Cam-
       bridge University Press, 1993), §50.

139   *duties without rights:* O'Neill, *Constructions of Reason* (Cam-
       bridge: Cambridge University Press, 1989), p. 179.

145   *source of value:* C. Korsgaard, *Creating the Kingdom of Ends*
       (Cambridge: Cambridge University Press, 1996), p. 124.

147   *ending that misery:* Ibid., p. 158.

147   *everyday lives:* Ibid., pp. 100–101.

151   *to pursue it:* Ibid., p. 126.

INDEX